MODERNISM

MODERNISM

A LITERATURE IN CRISIS

TERRY EAGLETON

YALE UNIVERSITY PRESS
NEW HAVEN AND LONDON

Permission to quote T.S. Eliot's 'A Cooking Egg', from *Collected Poems 1909–1962*, courtesy of Faber and Faber Ltd (UK and Commonwealth), courtesy HarperCollins Publishers (US and rest of the world)

Copyright © 2025 Yale University

All rights reserved. This book may not be reproduced in whole or in part, in any form (beyond that copying permitted by Sections 107 and 108 of the U.S. Copyright Law and except by reviewers for the public press) without written permission from the publishers.

All reasonable efforts have been made to provide accurate sources for all images that appear in this book. Any discrepancies or omissions will be rectified in future editions.

For information about this and other Yale University Press publications, please contact:
U.S. Office: sales.press@yale.edu   yalebooks.com
Europe Office: sales@yaleup.co.uk   yalebooks.co.uk

Set in Adobe Garamond Pro by IDSUK (DataConnection) Ltd
Printed and bound in the UK using 100% renewable electricity at CPI Group (UK) Ltd

Library of Congress Control Number: 2025935744
A catalogue record for this book is available from the British Library.
Authorized Representative in the EU: Easy Access System Europe, Mustamäe tee 50, 10621 Tallinn, Estonia, gpsr.requests@easproject.com

ISBN 978-0-300-28437-9

10 9 8 7 6 5 4 3 2 1

To Daniel, with love

CONTENTS

1	The Time of Modernism	1
2	Words and Things	59
3	The Death of Art	121
4	Conservative Revolutionaries	155
	Notes	*175*
	Index	*182*

1

THE TIME OF MODERNISM

The great outbreak of artistic experiment we know as modernism includes experiments with time, so it seems fitting that the word 'modernism' itself involves a twist of temporality. In its English usage, it did not become widely current until the 1960s, well after the highpoint of modernism itself.[1] By and large, the modernists did not think of themselves as modernists, any more than Dante thought of himself as medieval or the people of the so-called Dark Ages looked forward expectantly to being enlightened. The baptism of these eras was belated.

Modernism is not synonymous with 'modernity', a term which refers to the history of the last few centuries – though quite how far back it stretches is a controversial issue. Modernity has been variously dated from the Renaissance, the Reformation, the early seventeenth century and the eighteenth-century Enlightenment. Gutenberg, Columbus, Galileo, Luther and

Descartes have all been proposed for the role of founding father. We are speaking of the age of Protestantism and scientific rationalism, the rise of urbanism, industrial capitalism and the sovereign rights of private property, the emergence of the nation state and the advent of modern colonialism and imperialism. It is a time which also witnesses the ascent of liberal individualism, the evolution of democracy and civil rights, the growth of technology, the doctrines of progress and liberal democracy and the spread of secularisation.[2] Whether this epoch has now come to an end, yielding to the culture of postmodernism, or whether it remains an unfinished project, is a disputed question. Anyway, we shall see later that modernism and modernity are in some ways allies and in other ways antagonists.

Modernism was an astonishing outbreak of cultural innovation – one which spanned a range of different art forms and spread across a host of different nations, even if its artistic impact was strikingly disproportionate to its slender social base. It was largely confined to small coteries of artists and minority audiences, lasted no more than perhaps thirty years in its most fertile phase and, as Malcolm Bull remarks with an agreeable touch of hyperbole, was 'exclusively metropolitan, subsidised by eccentric millionaires and made by bohemians'.[3] Even so, some of its techniques were eventually to be appropriated by mass culture (film and advertising, for example) and to become familiar to millions of citizens who had never heard of Paul Klee or Georges Braque. Bull adds that modernism was never the culture of modernity as a whole, as postmodernism

THE TIME OF MODERNISM

can be described as the culture of postmodernity. Still, it represents one of the most vigorous flourishes of art since the Renaissance, which in its scope and originality, not to speak of its imaginative audacity, has never been equalled since. It swept from Brazil to Japan, Nigeria to Tibet, Turkey to Bengal.[4] With pardonable overstatement, Slavoj Žižek hails the movement as 'the only true artistic event of the twentieth century'.[5]

This global network existed alongside the growth of international monopoly capitalism and the international art market, even if it was frequently at odds with the values of both. Both capital and communism habitually cross national borders, and literature, too, was being prised free of provincialism, often by writers who had no secure footing in a single national culture. Ezra Pound's *The Cantos* (1917–68) is heavily freighted with allusions to Anglo-Saxon England, medieval Italy, ancient China and a prodigal span of other cultures, roaming freely in time and space. Ulysses, as Franco Moretti points out, is the Latin name for a Greek hero which provides the title of a novel by an Irishman who moved between Trieste, Zürich and Paris.[6]

Modernism in general stems from a historical crisis of immense proportions. Behind its most creative phase lies the lethal contention between imperialist powers commonly known as the First World War, an era which also witnessed severe economic depression, revolution in Russia and insurrection at the heart of Europe, a capitalist system in the throes of deep crisis, the rise of fascism and the exhilarating yet

MODERNISM

destabilising effect of new technologies. There is a general sense of anxiety and apocalypse abroad – of the collapse of older certainties, the destabilising of the self and the erosion of conventional mores. A liberal capitalism which affirms the individual spirit, feels assured of its own prosperity and looks confidently to the future is yielding ground to a monopoly capitalism marked by faceless bureaucracy, economic slumps, international conflict and the steady growth of mass culture. As the liberal centre ground crumbles, socialist forces confront governing classes which are being impelled increasingly to the political right. There is a dissolution of traditional bonds, along with a sense that history has stalled. Enlightenment ideals of peace, progress and emancipation lie in tatters at Ypres and the Somme, while the lived experience of individuals is increasingly one of solitude and alienation.

It is as though the human subject has imploded, lacking both a fixed centre and a stable foundation. Social reality appears opaque and anonymous, and individuals as mere functions of global powers beyond their control or comprehension. At the same time, the early twentieth century witnesses a rapid acceleration of technology along with a whole culture of innovation, so that if history is at a standstill it also appears to be racing recklessly forward. Modernism, with its breaks, fragments, elisions, obscurities, dissonances and multiple perspectives, is a set of strategies for representing this history, a task for which more conventional artistic techniques no longer seem adequate.

THE TIME OF MODERNISM

In a classic essay, Perry Anderson argues that the emergence of modernism requires three historical conditions. The first is the existence among societies still dominated by aristocratic or landowning classes of an established tradition of 'high' art and culture – a tradition on whose codes and techniques modernist art can draw, while at the same time rebelling against its inert academicism and patrician bias.[7] The second prerequisite is the overlapping of different historical modes of production or forms of social life, while the third is the proximity of political revolution. Modernist culture arises 'at the intersection between a semi-aristocratic ruling order, a semi-industrialised capitalist economy, and a semi-emergent, or -insurgent, labour movement'. Or, as Anderson encapsulates his case, modernism must have to hand 'a still usable classical past, a still indeterminate technical present, and a still unpredictable political future'.[8] Germany, for example, had become fully industrialised by the end of the First World War; yet there had been no equivalent change in its structures of power and culture, so that the nation remained largely hidebound and conservative. There was a disabling gap between its traditionalist moral values and the brutal mechanised warfare in which it had been recently engaged, an incongruity which the Dadaists and their artistic colleagues were not slow to exploit.

If modernism reaches its zenith in the years around the First World War, it is not least because the forces to which Anderson refers were then most intensively at work. What finally saw the movement off in his view was the Second World

MODERNISM

War, by which time the new technologies had become domesticated, the threat of revolution had receded, Europe was under reconstruction and the older aristocratic-agrarian order was in steep decline. In the modernist period, when technological development was still underway, it was not easy to predict its social and political outcome: would it usher in a utopia of leisure or a future of intensified labour? Would it prove exploitative or emancipatory? By the 1940s, the answer seemed clear enough. So-called Fordism or mass production arrived in Europe from the USA. The technological utopia of which the Futurists had dreamed turned out to be:

> an oppressively stable, monolithically industrial, capitalist civilisation . . . The ambiguity of aristocracy, the absurdity of academicism, the gaiety of the first cars or movies, the palpability of a socialist alternative, were all now gone. In their place, there now reigned a routinised, bureaucratised economy of universal commodity production, in which mass consumption and mass culture had become virtually interchangeable terms.[9]

Modernism, then, was for the most part exhausted; and though distinguished examples of such art continued to be produced, the heights scaled in the first few decades of the century were never to be attained again. In the end, modernist art was incorporated into the very bourgeois order it had despised, as Joyce entered the university syllabuses, Schoenberg sidled into the

THE TIME OF MODERNISM

concert hall and Abstract Expressionist canvases adorned the lobbies of US banks. Such artworks were now as canonical and institutionalised as the classical art they had repudiated. Even so, some of the conditions which had given birth to this culture were to re-emerge later in the post-colonial peripheries. It was to Gabriel García Márquez and Salman Rushdie that the Western nations were to look for much of their experimental fiction, not Hampstead or Manhattan.

Some modernist artworks sprang from specific movements (Futurism, Cubism, Expressionism, Surrealism and so on);[10] yet though there were numerous interactions between these currents, there could be some sharp contentions as well. There is little common ground between the anguished subjectivity of Expressionism and the spirit of rational analysis of Cubism, or between the technological triumphalism of Futurism and the anti-industrial bent of the Surrealists. Does modernism, then, have a coherent identity, or is it simply an empty signifier?

The answer is surely that it is neither a unified formation nor a set of purely disparate developments. It is rather a question of 'family resemblances' (to use Ludwig Wittgenstein's term) or a complex overlapping of features. There are indeed certain characteristics which crop up again and again: shock, dissonance, montage, fantasy, austerity, fragmentation, polyphony and impersonality, for example. Virginia Woolf speaks of the reader's need to 'tolerate the spasmodic, the obscure, the fragmentary, the failure'.[11] One might also list distortion,

MODERNISM

self-reflectiveness, irony, indeterminacy, the autonomy of the artwork, the isolation or dissolution of the self, non-linear narrative and multiple points of view. There is a fascination in some quarters with the 'primitive', atavistic, mystical, psychotic, libidinal, esoteric and mythological. Objects may appear opaque and enigmatic, while human subjects can feel shut off from each other in the prison cell of their privatised selves. Raymond Williams sees modernism as an 'intense, singular narrative of unsettlement, homelessness, solitude and impoverished independence'.[12] This is indeed true, though it passes over the pursuit of alternative forms of community as a reaction to this anomie, from D.H. Lawrence's Mexico to experiments in socialism and feminism.

Yet the features just listed are by no means restricted to modernism. Postmodernism can lay claim to quite a few of them, as can some realist art. Nor are all of them likely to be in evidence in a particular modernist work. It is not always easy to judge what counts as modernist writing, or who qualifies as a modernist author. W.B. Yeats, for example, is modernist in his elitism, right-wing radicalism, cyclical view of history, apocalyptic vision, preoccupation with myth, violence and the occult, Nietzschean individualism, contempt for the masses and desire to transcend history; but he is as thoroughly traditional in his verse forms as he is in some of his values, and his language is almost never ambiguous or indeterminate. One might claim that in that respect literary modernism proper is born when the forces of social disintegration begin

THE TIME OF MODERNISM

to invade the very forms of the artistic work – unlike, say, Alexander Pope's *The Dunciad* (1728–43), where it is part of the task of the trim heroic couplets to fend off the chaos they portray. Yeats, as we shall see later, is also a more public poet than most of his modernist colleagues.

'Modernism' is a polythetic term, meaning one which refers to a class of objects with a number of shared characteristics, but where no one of these characteristics is essential for membership of the class. ('Literature' is another such word.) There is no single property which all modernist works have in common, just as the various members of a family do not all need to have flaming-red hair or enormous ears in order to look alike. Yet to claim that there is in this sense no essence of modernism is not to suggest that all we have is a collection of unique particulars. The opposite of essentialism need not be pure difference, if such a thing exists. In fact, this is a mistake of which modernism itself is often culpable. If there are no longer any Platonic essences, so some thinkers suppose, then all must be flux and fragmentation. But these claims are simply sides of the same coin, the latter being an overreaction to the former. This is one reason why Martin Heidegger finds Friedrich Nietzsche a prisoner of metaphysics, though his work is all about flux and non-identity. Modernism is often to be found offering us a false choice between essentialism and nominalism, as indeed is its postmodern inheritor.[13]

It might be claimed that modernist works of art have a negative aspect in common, namely their attempt to break

MODERNISM

with realism. Modernism can be seen as a creative disfiguration of realism, a fact which for Georg Lukács's stiff-necked study *The Meaning of Contemporary Realism* counts heavily against it. For Lukács, modernism is really a bungled version of realism, one which has gone sour and shapeless. This overlooks the fact that modernist art can disfigure realism in illuminating ways as well as in objectionable ones. It can do so, however, only if it retains a trace of the realism it bends out of shape. To have force, a deviation has to call to mind the norm from which it departs. In this sense, modernism, despite its sometimes clamorous claims to originality, is unavoidably parasitic on realism, so that we would arguably be truly postmodernist only when we had become genuinely post-realist as well. Perhaps modernism bears something of the same relation to realism as dreams do to our waking life, at once divergent from and dependent on it, full of improbable fantasies yet drawing abundantly on everyday materials.

Modernism's reliance on realism is more than a formal affair. It goes to the very root of the modernist worldview. Classical realism, by and large, believes in a world with firm foundations and a meaningful structure – one in which truth and reality, though sometimes problematic, may be brought to light by patient investigation. The typical modernist work has had its faith in all of this badly shaken; but unlike its postmodern progeny it is old enough to recall (or to imagine that it recalls) a time when there was still truth, reality, foundations, transcendence and coherent identity, and to feel their

THE TIME OF MODERNISM

loss sorely. Something is lacking for modernism, so that many of its literary works seem to revolve around an absent centre. In Joseph Conrad's fiction, there is the unseen bomb explosion of *The Secret Agent* (1907), the silver of *Nostromo* (1904), the supposedly dark heart of Africa in *Heart of Darkness* (1899) and Jim's unrepresented jump from his ship in *Lord Jim* (1899–1900). There are the ghosts of Henry James's novella 'The Turn of the Screw' (1898) and the wild duck in Henrik Ibsen's play of that name (1884). One thinks, too, of the haunting absences at the heart of Rilke's writing, Wyndham Lewis's swirling vortices with their still centres or the Marabar Caves in E.M. Forster's *A Passage to India* (1924), along with the mysterious death of Mrs Moore in the same novel. The list could be extended to Virginia Woolf's lighthouse, the invisible authorities of Franz Kafka's *The Castle* (1926), the near-miss encounters of Stephen and Bloom in Joyce's *Ulysses* (1922), Samuel Beckett's perpetually absent Godot, the empty Chapel Perilous in *The Waste Land* (1922), the still point of the turning world in *Four Quartets* (1936–42) and so on.

All these are absences which, rather like the presence of some invisible planet, can be known by the way they wrench their surroundings out of shape. Reality has not exactly fallen to pieces, but there is an unsettling void at its centre. For postmodernism, by contrast, the disquieting sense that there is something lacking from reality, some primordial loss or flaw, is no more than a kind of phantom-limb syndrome or piece of clapped-out metaphysics. There never were any absolute

MODERNISM

truths, spiritual depths or ultimate foundations, so that the lack of them is no cause for anxiety. There is no point in scratching where it doesn't itch. What you see is what you get. If only we could remove the metaphysical spectacles from our nose, we would see that nothing is missing or concealed. We would also see that the world is no way in particular, and certainly no way which is distinct from our interpretations of it.

One might see the absences of modernism as signifiers of a missing totality – intimations of some momentous truth that vanishes whenever you try to look at it straight, like the figure who walks beside you in *The Waste Land*. Perhaps the Real, the True and the Self still exist, laid up in some Platonic heaven; but whereas classical realism has a vigorous faith that they can be accurately represented, modernism fails to share this conviction. Perhaps the work of art itself must be the new form of absolute value and ultimate reality, given that there seems not much else on offer; but how can it serve as a surrogate for these things precisely when it is at its most troubled and self-divided, thrown into permanent crisis and sceptical of its own right to exist?

If modernist art really was an assault on realism, however, the campaign was to prove singularly unsuccessful. Not only did realism continue to thrive during the period of high modernist art, but it carried on regardless once that era was over, as though nothing of great consequence had occurred. Realism, given its immensely rich history and general accessibility, is a peculiarly difficult mode to dislodge. One would

THE TIME OF MODERNISM

not guess from the fiction of Kingsley Amis or the poetry of Philip Larkin that they were written in the wake of a profound cultural crisis. One might note, however, that there is a good deal in the classical realist tradition from Balzac to Tolstoy that could scarcely be called realistic, just as a number of modernist writers would no doubt claim to be realist in some sense of the term deeper than the representation of everyday reality. It is not self-evidently absurd to call Kafka's *The Castle* or Faulkner's *The Sound and the Fury* realist, even if it is not particularly helpful either.

Can modernism really be confined to the early decades of the twentieth century? One might claim that it reached its peak between, say, Ezra Pound's poem 'The Seafarer' (1911) and James Joyce's *Finnegans Wake* (1939), three decades which constitute one of the most magnificent stretches of time in the whole of Western cultural history. Some scholars, however, allow modernist art a mere twenty years (1910–30), while others date it from 1890 to 1930, or 1890 to 1940.[14] A number of commentators see its demise as coinciding with the end of the Second World War, while for others it was dead on its feet before the first shot in that conflict was fired. If modernism is generally thought to have been exhausted by this point, it is not least because it was becoming gentrified or institutionalised, no longer a strain of cultural Bolshevism but a badge of Western freedom, enterprise and innovation. Yet T.J. Clark argues that in painting at least, modernism began in 1793 with the French artist David's painting of the death of

MODERNISM

Marat;[15] and what about Flaubert, Baudelaire, Rimbaud and Mallarmé? Are these modernist authors or modernist precursors? Arthur Rimbaud was calling for art to invent an absolutely new language as early as the 1870s. What of Symbolism, Impressionism, Naturalism, 'Decadence' and Aestheticism, much of which flourished before 1890?

Perhaps, then, one should date modernism from the mid-nineteenth century, at least as far as its French manifestations are concerned. Aestheticism can be traced back to the 1830s, with the work of Théophile Gautier, and was by no means a novelty even then. The modernist zest for innovation harks back even further, to the Romantic poets. A standard Marxist account, one favoured by the critic Georg Lukács in particular, traces the first stirrings of modernism to the period which follows the European insurrections of 1848, a date which in Lukács's view marks the watershed between the heroic, revolutionary phase of the middle class and its subsequent decline into irrationality and political reaction. This declension, as Lukács regards it, was later to take the form of fin-de-siècle Symbolism, Decadence and Aestheticism, which then played their part in fuelling later brands of twentieth-century modernism.

There are other problems of periodisation. If modernism ended around 1930, on the threshold of the Second World War or just after that event, having scaled its most spectacular peaks in the years around the so-called Great War, we still need to make room for the work of Samuel Beckett and the

THE TIME OF MODERNISM

aesthetics of the modernist critics Clement Greenberg and Maurice Blanchot, along with an army of other writers who continued to deploy modernist techniques into the 1950s and 1960s.[16] There is also the belated avant-gardism of the Situationists, who were to play a key role in the culture and politics of the late 1960s student movement.[17] A case can also be made that one of the latest upsurges of modernism is known as 'theory', which, from Adorno to Barthes, Blanchot to Derrida, preserves much of the modernist impulse and draws inspiration from some of its most eminent writers. Philosophers like Adorno and Derrida produce modernist texts, not simply reflections on modernist art.

Then there is the problem of postmodernism, which breaks with its predecessor in some ways while remaining faithful to it in others. Many of its forms and techniques echo modernist art, but in more vernacular, anti-elitist, post-metaphysical spirit. A good deal of what some see as peculiarly postmodern (irony, parody, playfulness, eclecticism, ungroundedness, self-reflexiveness, blending of 'high' and popular culture and so on) was already evident in some high modernism, which in this sense lives on in its more streetwise successor. In fact, it would not be entirely misleading to describe postmodernism as modernism shorn of its belief in the unity, purity, autonomy and transcendent aura of the work of art, which is admittedly to shed quite a bit of aesthetic baggage.

Perhaps 'modernism' is less a period term than a formally descriptive one, so that, say, Laurence Sterne's outrageously

MODERNISM

experimental, chronologically dishevelled novel *Tristram Shandy* (1759–67) could be granted the title. Some would claim the same for Georg Büchner's extraordinary drama *Woyzeck* (1836). In this sense, one might find modernist texts all the way back to the book of Jonah, rather as one might stumble across fragments of the Gothic or magic realism. There is a salutary reminder here that modernism does not always follow obediently on the heels of realism. In (post-)colonial nations in particular, a state of disjunction and fragmentation, of discrepant time schemes and cultural incongruities, may give rise to modernist works while the colonialist heartlands are still dominated by realist ones. On the whole, however, modernism in Europe and the United States denotes a historical period, whatever forerunners it may acknowledge and however much one might argue about when it starts and stops. If this is an ironic fact about it, it is because a good deal of modernist writing is thoroughly *un*historical, and would not be eager to be characterised as belonging to a particular phase of time. We shall be looking at this irony later.

Many modernist ideas are not new at all, not least the idea of the new. The word 'modern' derives, ironically enough, from the ancient term *modernus*, which became current in the medieval era and which means something like 'the time of the Now'. The Now, one should note, is not necessarily synonymous with the new. It means what is current or contemporary, much of which is not novel at all. Air travel is contemporary, but now has quite a history behind it. In one sense, 'the time

THE TIME OF MODERNISM

of the Now' smacks of the oxymoronic, since the Now is both in and out of time, no sooner here than gone, a sliver of temporality plucked from a ceaseless flow. Even if the Now is the new, the modern is actually rather long in the tooth, since it may be the fruit of a development that stretches far into the past. If one sees antiquity as the childhood of humanity, and modernity as its grown-up phase, then the modern is far from fresh and virginal.

Some modernist art (one thinks of T.S. Eliot's *Four Quartets*, or some of W.B. Yeats's work) seeks to immerse itself in perpetual flux while also transcending it, submitting to decay and mortality as the only means of entering upon the eternal, or grasping some precious moment which can be either frozen or endlessly perpetuated. Very little of this would have struck the Romantics as unfamiliar. Like Romanticism, modernism also tends to believe in originality, 'deep' subjectivity, the transcendent status of art, the idea of genius, the need for a spiritual elite, the uniqueness of the work of art and its antipathy to the marketplace. The faith of some Romantics that art can transform the world, however, is not typical of their modernist successors. There are also anti-Romantic modernists such as the Imagists, whose co-founder, along with Ezra Pound, was the American poet H.D. (Hilda Doolittle). Indeed, it may be that it was H.D.'s aesthetic theories which provided Pound with the ground for his poetic practice. Her poetry turns for the most part from the subject to the object, which is delineated with scrupulous exactness in lines so brief that they may travel only an inch or so across the page; yet there is also an erotic intensity at work in the verse.

In typical modernist style, H.D. yokes the ancient and the contemporary together: the occasion for her epic *Trilogy* is the Second World War, but the poem evokes Egyptian gods and the book of Revelation in the context of the turbulent present. As with *The Waste Land*, all wars are fundamentally one, as myth, parallelism and ritual repetition come to eclipse linear history.

An associate of the Imagists, though not, so to speak, a true believer, was the superbly accomplished Marianne Moore, who by the 1960s was widely recognised as America's most distinguished living poet. At the age of eighty she was granted an honour arguably more precious than the Nobel Prize, namely throwing out the first pitch to open the 1968 season in Yankee Stadium. Her work is marked by an austere elegance of language, rhythmical poise and formality of manner. Her poems have a remarkable precision of perception, but they are also more witty and discursive than the work of the Imagists, more hospitable to argument and abstraction. If they are more emotionally reticent than the work of H.D., they are also more complex and idiosyncratic in their use of language.

One visitor to the Bauhaus in Germany, one of the most renowned institutes of cultural experiment in the modernist period, wrote that 'the artistic climate here cannot support anything

THE TIME OF MODERNISM

that is not the latest, the most modern, up-to-the-minute, Dadism, circus, variety, jazz, hectic pace, movies, America, airplanes, the automobile'.[18] But a perpetual Now, or succession of absolutely original moments, dismantles all continuity, and along with it all enduring identity. If the self is reborn every second then there is nothing that persists, and thus nothing for perpetual renewal or innovation to happen to. True difference depends on a degree of consistency, and pure difference capsizes into pure identity. As with the paradoxes of the ancient philosopher Zeno of Elea, time becomes a series of disconnected moments, and thus ceases to flow at all. There is an image of such frozen temporality in Joseph Conrad's novel *The Secret Agent*, a work to which we shall be returning later:

> The cab rattled, jingled, jolted; in fact, the last was quite extraordinary. By its disproportionate violence and magnitude it obliterated every sensation of onward movement; and the effect was of being shaken in a stationary apparatus like a mediaeval device for the punishment of crime, or some very new-fangled invention for the cure of a sluggish liver.[19]

This sense of getting nowhere fast is the ultimate riposte to the ideology of progress, of which the conservative Conrad is deeply sceptical. How can there be progress when the very idea of motion is a metaphysical mystery? How can you be in one place at a particular moment yet at the same time en

MODERNISM

route to another? Conrad's cab passenger lives in an eternal present – a view of time, ironically, which can also be found in the classicism on which so much modernist art turns its back. The classical work may be less marooned in the past than perpetually up to date, contemporaneous with every historical situation. If it seems immune from decay, this might be because it can renew itself at every moment.[20] Its so-called timelessness may spring not from being sealed from temporality but from being constantly abreast of it.

When it comes to the question of innovation, there is an interesting ambiguity about Ezra Pound's celebrated slogan 'make it new!', which can mean either 'make something which is new' or 'renew what exists already'. The latter implies a degree of continuity, whereas the former does not. Total innovation cannot constitute a renewal, since the new can be gauged only by comparison with what precedes it. In any case, the new is not desirable in itself. Crack cocaine is relatively new, and so is failing to notice the murder of a fellow train passenger because you are too busy fiddling with your smartphone. Paul Valéry speaks of the idea of revolution in nineteenth-century France as 'the expression of an overturn of what currently exists as such, *whatever it is*. What matters becomes the change in itself.'[21] Difference outdoes repetition. Novelty and mutability are to be valued whatever their historical content. It is an emptily formalistic standpoint. Henri Bergson imports such avant-gardism into philosophy, claiming that 'duration means invention, the creation of forms, the continual elabora-

THE TIME OF MODERNISM

tion of the absolutely new'.[22] It is a case that will crop up again in the writings of Gilles Deleuze. The political philosopher Hannah Arendt maintains that the biological life process would bring everything to ruin were it not for the human capacity to interrupt it through action and initiate something unexpected. Humans, she writes, 'are not born in order to die but in order to begin'.[23]

What a new thing has in common with much of what surrounds it is precisely its novelty, so that innovation risks becoming as stalely familiar as narcissism in the entertainment industry. 'The pleasure which we derive from the representation of the present', writes Charles Baudelaire, 'is due not only to the beauty with which it can be invested, but also to its essential quality of being present.'[24] And for this poet, the present means the new. It is not just contemporary reality but the *fact* that it is contemporary which is so alluring. The finest art has a quality over and above its value or content, namely its up-to-dateness. Yet famine and sexual slavery may also be the latest thing. Moreover, just as the present is precious in itself, so modernism can regard the past with suspicion simply because it is the past, not because of any specific offence that it may have committed. As Joshua Cohen puts it in his novel *The Netanyahus* (2021), the past on this view is merely the process by which the present is attained. Its value is purely instrumental.

It is with Baudelaire that the idea of the modern as the fugitive, fleeting and contingent is born. What is most distinctive about modern experience is that it constitutes a perpetual

MODERNISM

vanishing act. The present moment is so fragile and evanescent than it can be conceptually grasped only when it has disappeared. 'The present', writes Wyndham Lewis, 'cannot be revealed to people until it has become yesterday.'[25] One spurns what has gone before in the name of a present which is even now merging with the future and fading into oblivion. The very term 'Futurism' suggests that the present itself is obsolete. This has some unsettling implications for traditional art, whose apologists have often enough seen permanence as a supreme measure of its worth. In some avant-garde circles, by contrast, the ephemeral is not only accepted but eagerly embraced. Why not scribble your poems on people's shirtfronts, or build a self-implosive device into your sculpture? What is so admirable about durability? Torture and destitution have been persistent factors in human history, yet we do not think the better of them for that. Besides, a perishable art is less easily institutionalised. The problem is that to place a heap of rotten turnips in an art gallery once may be subversive, whereas to do it twice is to risk establishing a tradition. And tradition is not what most modernist artists look upon benignly.

For Baudelaire and some of his fellow modernists, the Now is a form of eternity secreted at the heart of temporality. Like eternity, it is timeless, so that these two apparent opposites share a secret affinity. Each moment of time is symbolic of the whole or Absolute: as James Joyce's Stephen Dedalus declares, one must cling to the now and the here, through which all future plunges to the past. In a similar way, every aspect of the

THE TIME OF MODERNISM

world can become a microcosm of everything else, so that symbolism – revealing the whole in the part – is somehow built into it. On this view, each thing is what it is only because of the exact mode of existence of all the others. One minor adjustment to the cosmos would transfigure everything. What seems fleeting and incidental thus has a secret law-like necessity about it. As the philosopher Georg Simmel writes, 'the typical is to be found in what is unique, the law-like in what is fortuitous, the essence and significance of things in the superficial and transitory.'[26] If this is so, then the ephemeral, unstable nature of the modern need not be as catastrophic as it seems. Yet whereas for the Romantics and Idealists the Absolute can become incarnate in a symbol, or even in an extraordinary figure or event, the modernists are plagued by a sense of its evasiveness – by their inability, in the words of the poet Edward Thomas, to 'bite the day to the core'.[27]

There may, however, be a way of using language which allows you to leap beyond it to a realm of timeless truth. On this view, words are authentic only when they are self-negating, leaving in their wake a dim intimation of what can be shown but not said. The aim of such self-abolishing artworks is to gesture to their own limits – to the borders where they tail off into the inarticulate, the resonant silences concealed at their core. By drawing attention to these boundaries, art allows us a negative glimpse of the infinity which lies beyond them. It gives rise to a sudden epiphany or inexplicable rupture in the Real, through which we can glimpse the profile of God or the

MODERNISM

Meaning of meanings. This, in effect, was the faith of Symbolists such as Stéphane Mallarmé.

Such revelation is possible only through the medium of language, but the recalcitrance of words is also what frustrates it. Determinate meaning must therefore be dissolved, so that poetry becomes a language which speaks with remarkable eloquence of its inability to express what it means. Having failed to gain access to the Absolute, one must, in Eliot's phrase, launch yet another futile raid on the inarticulate; and it is in this continual attempt to outflank the treachery of words, this process of perpetually falling back yet failing better, that literature is born. If modernist art is self-defeating, it is because it is seized by a passion for the Real which it knows to be impossible, and is thus ironic in its very form. The most it can achieve is to name its own bafflement in striving for what eludes it.

Perhaps if one were finally to close one's fist over the Now, Here or Real, to capture in a single image whatever trauma, *jouissance*, miracle or unclean thing lurks at the core of reality, history would come to an end. Either that, or the poet would have absolutely nothing left to say. That the Real (meaning something like the truth of human desire) lies beyond representation is a recurrent motif of modernism, as it is for that most mandarin of late modernists, the psychoanalyst Jacques Lacan. Yet the Real is not to be mistaken for anything as pedestrian as everyday reality, a sphere which for psychoanalysis exists to protect us from the Real, and which for a modernist

24

THE TIME OF MODERNISM

aesthetic can be delegated to greengrocers and naturalistic novelists.

Modernism, then, seeks to place time and eternity in a complex relation with one another, in contrast to a postmodernism for which the eternal simply drops off the screen. Postmodernism may find a certain value in the new, but unlike its modernist forebears it does not come up with a metaphysics of innovation. It is too fond of the repetitive, derivative and recycled to do that, which is to say too much in thrall to the commodity form. Some of its modernist forerunners aim to defeat history by compressing time into an infinite singularity. Or they may try to tear a gap in the fabric of the temporal, through which eternal mythologies or the collective unconscious may come welling up. The modernist fascination with the void or vortex, 'vertical' irruptions into the flow of temporality, belongs with this vision. So do attempts to 'spatialise' time, as with Walter Benjamin's project of 'constellating' different fragments of history in a single image.[28] As one's faith in history falters, the linear gives way to the synchronic, movement to montage, time to space.

One source of this shift is the city, the home territory of modernism, in which different sensations besiege you from all sides at every instant. A number of modernist artists hailed from rural, provincial, economically undeveloped societies with conservative mores and authoritarian states, and so were understandably enraptured by the freedoms and fulfilments of the metropolis.[29] It is the city, at once disruptive and enthralling,

MODERNISM

with what Walter Benjamin calls its 'inconceivable analogies and connections between events',[30] which stirs modernism's interest in random affinities and incongruous juxtapositions. Dorothy Richardson's epic novel *Pilgrimage*, which was published in thirteen volumes from 1915 to 1967, unfolding throughout the whole modernist period and well beyond it, finds urban life both inspiring and overwhelming. The simultaneity of urban experiences becomes fashionable when one's trust in historical evolution begins to flag.

Behind modernism lies an age of war and revolution so deeply traumatising that it calls into question the very meaning of history itself, as the mighty era of bourgeois progress appears to unravel before one's eyes and civilisation at its zenith begins to slide back into barbarism. Another source of the modernist aversion to the linear is modern physics, for which a Newtonian world of solid objects, fixed laws of causality and single-track temporality is yielding to an indeterminate, multidimensional domain of energy and mutation. Time for Albert Einstein's special theory of relativity does not run on rails, which is no doubt why some of the Dadaists, who preferred the synchronic to the evolutionary, regarded him as an honorary member of their movement, along with Charlie Chaplin.

If you want to defeat the time of clocks and calendars, which is the province of bureaucrats and politicians, you can also try turning inward to the 'lived', irregular, multilayered temporality of the human subject, which tends to spill over

THE TIME OF MODERNISM

the edges of any strictly linear scheme. Interior time, which can loop back on itself, split into criss-crossing tributaries, leap suddenly forward or appear to stand still, does not respect the laws of chronology. In philosophy, this trend takes the form of phenomenology. Its finest literary manifestation is Marcel Proust's *Remembrance of Things Past* (1913–27). Alternatively, you can adopt the Futurist tactic of trying to outrun time, beating it at its own game by ensuring that you are always out ahead of it, so that past and present are continually eclipsed by the promise of what is still to come. Even the contemporary is now obsolete. The present is sheer deferment, an empty excited openness to a future which has in one sense already arrived, in another sense is yet to materialise and in yet another sense will never emerge other than as the instantly superseded moment of the contemporary. Time moves at such a speed that it warps and buckles, as the present becomes the first day of the future. If you cannot transcend temporality, you can at least intensify it, opening up depths and discontinuities beneath its apparently unfractured surface. In market conditions, you have to run very fast to stay on the spot where you are. In psychoanalytic terms, the impulse which scoops out the present for a future which will instantly evaporate is known as desire, a major motif of the Surrealists.

It may be, however, that you are driven forward less by a hunger for the future than by a weariness with the past. 'What drives modernism to innovate', remarks Fredric Jameson, 'is not some vision of the future or the new, but rather the deep

MODERNISM

conviction that certain forms and expressions, procedures and techniques, can no longer be used, are worn out or stigmatised by their associations with a past that has become conventionality or kitsch, and must be creatively avoided.'[31] Some strains of modernism, to be sure, nurture visions of the future; but Jameson is right to see that modernist artists are among other things in revolt against the hackneyed and humdrum. Staleness and tedium are among their deadliest enemies.

Alternatively, you can resist the headlong flow of history, not least the discredited doctrine of progress, by looping temporality back upon itself – either in the nostalgic style of Proust, or in a cyclical vision which takes its cue from Friedrich Nietzsche's doctrine of eternal recurrence. Yeats's gyres and James Joyce's Viconian cycles are cases in point. In an interplay of difference and identity, time and eternity, everything that has ever happened will eventually return, perhaps in an unfamiliar guise. For Joyce, history, indeed the entire cosmos, consists of a fixed set of features which continually enter into new combinations, rather like the alphabet. The same is true for structuralist theory, which has its origins in the modernist era. Nothing is ever genuinely new, then; but nothing is ever exactly repeated either, not least because it has happened once already. It is a vision suitable for an age of fashion and the commodity, which are perpetually repackaged but never fundamentally transformed. 'Never-changing ever-changing', as Joyce remarks of the sea in *Ulysses*. Novelty is just the same old thing. It can also be hard to distinguish the innovative from

THE TIME OF MODERNISM

the antique, not least because what has not happened for a long time is as unfamiliar as what was created five minutes ago.

More plausibly, you can argue that history is a multiple, diffuse affair rather than a monolithic narrative – that any contemporary moment is bound to contain a rich array of conflicting mini-narratives which are by no means always smoothly synchronised. It is a view more persuasive on the colonial margins than the metropolitan centre. Different currents of history move at different tempos, diverge or randomly intersect, curve back on themselves or suddenly accelerate, as the structure of Conrad's novel *Nostromo* would suggest. You may still imagine history as surging forward, yet hold with the philosopher Oswald Spengler in his *The Decline of the West* (1918–22) that there comes a point where every civilisation starts inexorably to decline – the doctrine of so-called decadence. If those decadent modernist artists who revel in the dissolute and exotic are anything to judge by, the slope downward can be quite as gratifying as the climb upward.

If history is less linear than multilayered, you can shake its various bits and pieces free of their chronological frame and slice into it at any point. Everything is perpetually present to a certain modernist eye, just as everything is eternally present to the mind of God. The possibility of a surrealist history, one which brings the old and the new into shocking juxtapositions, arrives on the agenda. So also, however, does the possibility of a conservatism which regards history as a form of

MODERNISM

eternity in the sense that nothing fundamentally alters. *The Waste Land* is informed by such a view, though it also hints at the alternative (and incompatible) conservative case that history does indeed change, but only in the sense of it steadily deteriorating.

Some of the revolutionary avant-gardes sought to wipe the slate clean of all previous history in order to create a luminous space for their own ground-breaking art. Each artist is a species of demi-god, fashioning their own universe in the hope that its flawlessness will improve on God's own miserably defective handiwork. Yet the fact is that there is no such thing as absolute innovation, since (as postmodernism concedes more readily than modernism) everything from literary texts to the Bank of England is manufactured out of pre-existent materials, and is to that extent derivative. There is no creation ex nihilo, an act which is the preserve of the Almighty rather than of minuscule bands of modernists. In the beginning was the copy. How can one make a fresh start other than with the compromised, contaminated stuff which the past has bequeathed us? How could we articulate something so utterly new as to transcend our current frames of reference, and yet still be capable of identifying it? History, for both good and ill, is what we are made of. Most of the past does not exist, any more than the future does; but as Henrik Ibsen suspects, it is always likely to outweigh the present simply because there is so much more of it. Works of art which try to liquidate the past tend to overlook Freud's warning that those who do not

THE TIME OF MODERNISM

confront it are doomed to repeat it. All you are likely to do is to thrust the past into the political unconscious, where it may begin to fester.

If you are feeling really reckless, you can try to put a bomb under time itself in order to blow a black hole in the stuff, as with the demented Professor of Conrad's *The Secret Agent*. This, however, is not a simple matter, since history is gross, material stuff which has an unnerving habit of creeping back into place once one has tried to dislodge it. Such, at least, is the London of Conrad's novel, a dank, fog-bound city whose streets have 'the majesty of inorganic nature, of matter that never dies'. A police constable seems to surge out of a lamp-post, as though he, too, were part of inorganic nature. The novel's vision, deeply influenced by literary naturalism, is of an oozy, viscous city populated by grotesque, object-like figures, which it would take more than a bomb to blow apart. This is one reason why the work cannot decide whether its anarchist characters are ludicrous or alarming. When the book's chief protagonist, Mr Verloc, ventures out of his house,

> his descent into the street was like the descent into a slimy aquarium from which the water had been run off. A murky, gloomy dampness enveloped him.
>
> The walls of the houses were wet, the mud of the roadway glistened with an effect of phosphorescence, and when he emerged into the Strand out of a narrow street by

MODERNISM

the side of Charing Cross station, the genius of the locality assimilated him. He might have been but one more of the queer foreign fish that can be seen of an evening about there flitting round the dark corners.

The anarchists in the novel may dream of a new humanity, but the book presents humans as mere outcroppings of nature, interchangeable with the lower animals. The corpulent Mr Verloc is built of such solid stuff (like 'a fat rock') that it is a mystery how he moves. A young boy, Stevie, is blown to bits by a bomb, but tell-tale pieces of his body and clothing survive like 'a heap of rags, scorched and bloodstained, half concealing what might have been an accumulation of raw material for a cannibal feast'. Reality is too dense to be destroyed, and human existence is just an endless recycling of meaningless matter in slightly variable forms. It is precisely because it is so brute, so void of meaning and value, that the world persists – a fact which, were they to be aware of it, would be no source of consolation to its inhabitants. Fortunately, however, they are not. For Conrad, as for a number of his fellow modernist artists, everyday consciousness is false consciousness.

The Professor is the perfect anarchist because he wants to annihilate not just this or that institution, but civilisation, even reality itself. Only then could one make a genuinely fresh start. If matter is as intractable as it is, the only effective transfiguration would have to be an absolute one. This malevolent figure, then, is not only the perfect anarchist but the archetyp-

THE TIME OF MODERNISM

al avant-gardist. Whatever exists must be wiped away, in an ecstatic act of destruction which is also a perverse form of creation. It is the only way one can get on equal terms with God, as a dark parody of his bringing the world into being in the first place. There are few more erotic forms of fulfilment than the death drive; and to destroy, as every toddler knows, can be quite as gratifying as to create. 'I depend on death,' the Professor declares, 'which knows no restraint and cannot be attacked. My superiority is evident.' His desire is to see 'death enlisted for good and all in the service of humanity', sweeping people out of the way like so much rotten garbage so that a utopian future may replace them. It is a classic avant-gardist fantasy. Other revolutionaries, he scoffs, seek to derive the future from the present, whereas he himself wants 'a clean sweep and a clear start for a new conception of life'. There will be no laborious process of reform, which is bound to involve complicity with what one wishes to overturn. Instead, this crazed nihilist, who lives in some liminal state between life and death, stalks around permanently wired up with explosives. Impossible to 'outleft', he is in search of the perfect detonator, which will despatch himself and his surroundings to eternity in a split second should he be threatened with arrest.

Unfortunately for Conrad's anarchists, however, time can no more be eclipsed than matter can be obliterated. Verloc arranges for a bomb to be placed at Greenwich Observatory, the prime meridian or still point of the turning world, as though he wants to tear through the very fabric of time itself;

MODERNISM

but the attempt is bungled and history refuses to come to a halt. You cannot leap in one bound from the finite to the infinite, as some modernist art likes to dream. To trigger his bomb, the Professor needs to press a small rubber ball he carries in his pocket, but the device involves a twenty-second lag before the explosion occurs. Instant eternity is impossible to come by. Time can be made to stand still for a moment, as when the long-suffering Mrs Verloc buries a knife in her brute of a husband's chest; but she is soon to hear the sound of a steady dripping of blood, 'like the pulse of an insane clock', which signifies that process, temporality and organic dissolution are once again under way. One can somersault for a precious moment out of history, but history will then reclaim you, rather as one who jumps from a height experiences a momentary freedom before falling victim to the forces of gravity. Mrs Verloc spends the rest of her time in the novel as a terrified victim of her sole authentic act, while the Professor's freedom consists in being prepared to exterminate himself. In the act of suicide, as a Dostoevsky character comments, one becomes godlike, supremely sovereign over one's own existence. To live permanently with one's death is to disarm it. Yet the consequence of the Professor's freedom will be literally nothing.

The perfect anarchist is also the perfect Dadaist. What is one to say, asks one character in the novel, of 'an act of destructive ferocity so absurd as to be incomprehensible, inexplicable, almost unthinkable; in fact, mad? Madness alone is truly terrifying.' The attack 'must have all the shocking senselessness of

34

THE TIME OF MODERNISM

gratuitous blasphemy'. There could be few more accurate descriptions of that sector of the avant-garde which is out to emancipate itself not only from bourgeois respectability but from the manacles of meaning itself. To be intelligible is to be in collusion with the bankers and bureaucrats. Perhaps it is senselessness that the ruling powers find hardest to stomach. Maybe absurdity is more subversive than storming Capitol Hill. At their nightclub in Zürich during the First World War, a city which was also home at the time to James Joyce and Vladimir Lenin, the Dadaists declaimed poems in different languages simultaneously and thumped on outsized drums, while the artist Hugo Ball delivered so-called phonetic poetry based on sound rather than sense while dressed in a magician's costume made of cardboard. Strident, outrageous, insulting and buffoonish, Dada later launched a nightclub in Berlin in which various surreal events were staged, including a race between a typewriter and a sewing machine.

The Secret Agent is among other things an allegory of the modernist artist. In anti-modernist spirit, all attempts at absolute originality come to grief; but the main reason why they do so – the dull persistence of a seedy, degenerate world – involves the kind of disdainful view of everyday life which many a modernist adopted. The novel is thus modernist and anti-modernist at the same time: social existence is worthless, but those who seek to destroy and reconstruct it are freaks and madmen. The Professor finally walks off, detonator in pocket, 'like a pest in the street full of men'; but elsewhere the work

35

MODERNISM

would seem to take a view of these urban crowds very close to the Professor's own:

> He was in a long, straight street, peopled by a mere fraction of an immense multitude; but all round him, on and on, even to the limits of the horizon hidden by the enormous piles of bricks, he felt the mass of mankind mighty in its numbers. They swarmed numerous like locusts, industrious like ants, thoughtless like a natural force, pushing on blind and orderly and absorbed, impervious to sentiment, to logic, to terror, too, perhaps.

The Professor's elitist disdain for the masses, typical of certain strains of modernism, would seem here to merge with the author's own. In one sense, it is salutary in Conrad's view that everyday existence is so sluggish and recalcitrant, since this means that madcap revolutionary schemes to reconstruct it must inevitably founder; yet at the same time this torpor is scarcely a reason for rejoicing. We are offered a choice between a dingy but reassuring English normality and a fascinating but repellent Continental fanaticism. The reader is allowed nowhere else to stand. Either you refuse to look too deeply into things (the workaday philosophy of Mrs Verloc), or like the Professor you glare through a paper-thin human existence to the seductive abyss which underlies it.

If the Professor is a modernist artist, so also is young Stevie. As an intellectually disabled child, he has trouble with lan-

THE TIME OF MODERNISM

guage, rather like some modernist writers; but though he is almost wordless, he is able through his obsessively scribbled drawings to catch a glimpse of the infinite. We see him sitting at a table 'drawing circles, circles, circles; innumerable circles, concentric, eccentric; a coruscating whirl of circles that by their tangled multitude of repeated curves, uniformity of form, and confusion of intersecting lines suggested a rendering of cosmic chaos, the symbolism of a mad art attempting the inconceivable'. Blown to pieces at the prime meridian, Stevie seeks in his scribblings to break with linearity and annihilate time. He is a compassionate child, deeply distressed by the world's inhumanity, and it may be that his whorls and cycles hint in Symbolist fashion at an eternity that would provide some utopian recompense for the cruelties of the present. In Wittgensteinian phrase, these compulsive scrawlings represent the mystical, which can be shown but not said. In the end, however, history in Conrad's view will wreak its revenge on all such noble aspirations, as we shall see when we come to consider the fate of the avant-garde.

Trying to efface the past is itself an historical event, and thus piles yet more material on what it aims to expunge. Attempts to break out of history, like proclamations that it is over, have an embarrassingly long history. There is a venerable tradition of breaks with tradition, rather as the idea of novelty stretches back to antiquity. For a critic like Paul de Man, modern literature is nothing less than this constantly doomed, ironically

MODERNISM

self-undoing attempt to make it new, this inability ever quite to awaken from the nightmare of history. 'The continuous appeal of modernity,' de Man comments, 'the desire to break out of literature toward the reality of the moment, prevails and, in turn, folding back on itself, engenders the repetition and continuation of literature.'[32] In this jaundiced view, to write in modernist style is to shatter a tradition that depends on such disruptions for its very self-reproduction. We may try to confront the Real or the Now eyeball to eyeball, but the very medium which facilitates this encounter – language, form, literary convention – is also likely to obstruct it.

De Man's claim is true of modernism in one obvious sense, as – much of it does indeed end up entering the very literary canon which it disparages. Why did this come about? Why does the transgressive become institutionalised? The prime target for modernism's shock tactics was the European haute bourgeoisie, which was cultivated enough to value art but respectable enough to be outraged by outré versions of it. Its inheritors, however, for whom such improprieties had become familiar, proved to be less easily scandalised. They also came to regard modernism as a badge of social status, not least when its tumultuous political context had faded from memory. As Stefan Collini remarks, 'high culture, high modernism, and high social class were . . . closely associated.'[33] Cultural capital went hand in hand with social and economic capital. In our own time, these people have given way in their turn to a new kind of middle class – an amorphous bunch of

THE TIME OF MODERNISM

technocrats, financiers, chief executives, IT experts, TV producers and publicity agents who have little appetite for art and are by no means in hot pursuit of high-cultural status. Nor do they typically have the skill or leisure to decipher artworks which are demanding. As a result of this and other factors, modernism survives mostly in academia.

Much of this art regards itself as breaking with the whole of previous history, which is part of what the word 'modern' is meant to signify. It is not simply that we have shifted to a new phase of time, but that this particular moment of history renders obsolescent everything that precedes it. The act of initiating a new era is also a gesture of repudiation, consigning the past to a nameless void. 'Modernity', observes Peter Osborne, 'is a form of forgetting.'[34] It is an antiquating force. What is truly original must be self-creating, sprung from its own loins, since to acknowledge a progenitor is to concede that one is leashed ineluctably to the past. The modern, by contrast, violently expels the past to a non-place and non-time, opening up an unbridgeable gulf between itself and its ancestors. In doing so, it tends to homogenise what has gone before, since the only difference that really counts is the contrast between the past as a whole and the moment of the modern. If modernity refuses to see itself simply as one historical period among others, it is because to do so would be to level itself with a heritage it is out to demolish.

What is at stake here among other things is the wholesale destruction of tradition (much of it quite recently invented) in

39

MODERNISM

a capitalist order that can find little use for it apart from 'heritage', museum piece or decorative window dressing. Some of those who discard tradition in the name of independent thought find their philosophical fathers in Descartes and Kant, both of whom wrestled with intellectual legacies which seemed to thwart this freedom. Yet the great majority of people in history have lived by tradition, which is to say by being loyal to the values and beliefs of their predecessors. This is not necessarily a conservative posture. Your ancestors might have spent their time organising armed rebellion against injustice. There are radical traditions as well as reactionary ones. If there is the House of Lords and fagging at Eton, there are also the Chartists and suffragettes. When Walter Benjamin speaks of tradition in his 'Theses on the Philosophy of History', it is the lineage of the oppressed – of those slain in their strike for justice in the past – that he has in mind.

In any case, though what millions of people have believed over long periods of time is by no means invariably true, it is likely to be a surer guide to the truth than a bright idea dreamt up in the small hours by some solitary intellectual. For many modernists, however, history is no longer a source of wisdom or set of instructive precedents. It is rather, as Joyce's Stephen Dedalus remarks, a nightmare from which they are trying to awaken; and with the horror of the First World War this nightmare breaks violently into their waking lives as well. The true nightmare may be to imagine that one has woken up only to discover by some slippage of sense or slight warping of

THE TIME OF MODERNISM

perception that one is still asleep. Many a political revolution, including in some respects the one which took place in Ireland at the time of *Ulysses'* appearance, has known such a false awakening.

Modernism may be wary of tradition, but there is a current within it which is in love with the archaic and atavistic. If some versions of it look to a brave new world, others gaze back to a more pristine past. And there are also plenty of modernists who look both ways at the same time. T.S. Eliot once remarked that the poet must be at once the most primitive and sophisticated of individuals. If *The Waste Land* is the latest thing in poetic experiment, it is also covertly shaped by ancient mythologies. Its path-breaking author is also the rather prim conservative of the essay 'Tradition and the Individual Talent' (1919), which was published only a few years earlier. The Dadaist poet Tristan Tzara was eager to fuse 'primitive' technique with modern sensibility. If you are disenchanted with the modern age, you can always try to leap ahead of it into some as yet unnameable future, like Rupert Birkin in D.H. Lawrence's *Women in Love* (1920). But you can also turn back to a blessed moment before its onset: to the so-called organic rural society, 'primitive' mythologies, ninth-century Byzantium, medieval China, the era of the gods or the rule of the warriors and feudal barons who thrived before our calamitous fall into commercialism. Some of H.D.'s writings, not least in the three long poems of *Trilogy*, excavate the ancient civilisations of Egypt and Mesopotamia, while other

41

MODERNISM

works of hers turn to classical antiquity. The more rationalistic, technocratic modernist artists, from the Russian Constructivists to the German Bauhaus, glance back not to the ancient or medieval but to the Enlightenment. Some of their critics, however, claim that the apparently progressive doctrines of this movement – Reason, Progress, Equality, Science – are themselves no more than myths robed in secular garb, and in this sense as retrograde as a reversion to Aztec deities or morris dancing.

There are a number of what one might call archaic avant-gardes in the modernist era, for which blood cults and arcane rites are the latest thing. Past and present interlock: as the narrator of Joseph Conrad's *Heart of Darkness* journeys forward into the heart of Africa, he is simultaneously moving backwards into some unspeakably 'savage' past. W.B. Yeats glimpses the shades of mythological Irish heroes shoulder to shoulder with the rebels of Easter 1916. If J.M. Synge was a mythologist of the time-hallowed Aran islands, he was also an habitué of bohemian Parisian cafes. 'So we beat on, boats against the current, borne back ceaselessly into the past,' reads the final sentence of F. Scott Fitzgerald's *The Great Gatsby* (1925). You can look back over the head of a bankrupt modernity in order to find the future in the primeval. From this standpoint, the modern period might appear as no more than a regrettable interlude between the two. Perhaps the whole era of rationalism and individualism was a temporary aberration, and we are now in the process of returning to the bosom of

THE TIME OF MODERNISM

our ancestors, drawing upon their numinous powers in order to build a future.

If the individual ego is felt to be in pieces, new forms of subjectivity might be discovered in the communal and impersonal. They can be glimpsed in the communism of the future, but also in the tribal collectivities of the past. The present must turn its face to the past if the future is to flourish, drawing on its vital energies and pre-rational wisdom. In Freud's view, one must confront the trauma of one's individual past in order to move forward into a future free of neurosis. Walter Benjamin's 'Theses on the Philosophy of History' portrays the Angel of History as blown backwards into the future, his horror-stricken gaze fixed on the mounting pile of garbage that is the past. Benjamin himself was to meet his death at the hands of another form of archaic avant-gardism: fascism. Fascism is a full-bloodedly modernist invention, facing both backwards and forwards simultaneously. If it marches robotically into a brand new technological age, mesmerised by the vision of a mechanised post-humanity, it does so while celebrating myth, the occult, astrology, blood and soil, the ancient racial origins of the People, medieval knights and the return of the pagan gods. Mass mechanisation and dabblings in the black arts strike up curious affinities. In our own time, we have witnessed yet another conjunction of the modern and archaic, as age-old mythologies are pressed into the service of political terror.

If some modernist works draw the very old and the very new into strange alliances, modernism itself springs from

MODERNISM

conditions which are just of this kind. It has been seen as the result of an incomplete or uneven process of modernisation – one in which the new is emerging with explosive force, but against the backdrop of a social order which remains in some ways stable and customary. In such a context, the modern appears more beguiling, but also more unnerving, than it does in societies more accustomed to rapid change. As Fredric Jameson writes, 'Apollinaire's Paris included both grimy medieval monuments and cramped Renaissance tenements, *and* motor cars and airplanes, telephones, electricity, and the latest fashions in clothing and culture. You know and experience these last as new and modern only because the old and traditional are also present.'[35] It is as though different strata of time are stacked together to produce the most contrary effects: 'handicrafts alongside the great cartels, peasant fields with the Krupp factories or the Ford plant in the distance'.[36] In postmodern societies, by contrast, where the modernising process is complete, the new is nothing new. Once novelty eclipses tradition altogether, the clash of cultures on which modernist art thrives itself becomes ancient history, and we have entered the era of postmodernity.

An incomplete modernity is nowhere more evident than in colonial and post-colonial nations, where customary forms of life may be overlaid with the quite different temporality of modern capitalism. The result in literary terms may be a world of myth and fantasy, fractured or traumatised selves, narrative disruption, a clash of linguistic idioms, the collision of the

THE TIME OF MODERNISM

new with the traditional and a hallucinatory sense of unreality. As a commentary on world literature puts it, such works employ 'various technical devices conventionally associated with modernism – digressions, restlessly shifting viewpoints, subversions of conventional causality, chronological disjunction, discursiveness – the form of the novel gestures to the uneven results of forced integration to the modern world-system.'[37] Ironically, what catapults you into a form of modernism is your very 'backwardness', rather as the weakness of capitalist modernity in Russia, not least the absence of a well-developed civil society, helped to produce a 'modern' socialist revolution in 1917.

If Western modernism imports various racist stereotypes of the primitive, exotic and Oriental to revitalise a jaded civilisation, it also exports its own artistic products to the colonial margins. At the same time, some of those peripheral nations give birth to their own indigenous forms of modernist culture, which interact with strains shipped in from elsewhere. Modernism implants itself in the colonial world as a form of Western hegemony; but just as it can provide a critique of modernity within the West, so can it also on the colonial edges, where modern ideas of progress, enlightenment, material prosperity and the self-determining human subject are not hard to unmask as partial or even bankrupt. In this situation, the language of modernity clashes or combines with more traditional forms and idioms to help breed a modernist art; but that self-assured modern vision is increasingly in trouble in its

MODERNISM

own homelands, and modernist culture is among other things a response to this predicament.

The highpoint of modernist art coincides with the point at which the British Empire reaches its maximum size, and imperialism in general is at its most expansionist and aggressive.[38] As a Janus-faced phenomenon, modernism can play its part in anti-colonial struggles at the same time as it diffuses colonialist values to regions which are still in part pre-modern. It is an ambiguity which can be found within particular literary works. Joseph Conrad's *Heart of Darkness* undercuts colonialist pretensions by exposing Kurtz, avatar of Western enlightenment, as corrupt to the core, but it is 'dark' Africa which has infected him with the virus of nihilism. E.M. Forster's *A Passage to India* satirises the imperialist project in the subcontinent, but partly because the novel connives in the patronising Western view that India is formless, opaque and therefore ungovernable.

If modernism reconfigures time, it does something similar with space. With modernism, geography comes into its own. Only a handful of the most eminent British modernist writers were indigenous to the country. Of those that were, two of the most prominent were hardly typical products of the British cultural establishment. One was a radical feminist married to a Jewish socialist (Woolf), while the other was the son of a provincial coalminer who abandoned England to roam the globe (Lawrence). Resistant to the modernist venture, Britain

46

THE TIME OF MODERNISM

had to import most of its experimental writers from abroad. In the late nineteenth century, 'Decadence', Naturalism, Symbolism and Aestheticism were shipped from France to be seized on by such louche figures as Oscar Wilde and Aubrey Beardsley. Modernism was mostly the concoction of foreigners – and in insular, imperial Britain, foreigners were not for the most part popular figures. Free verse seemed as anti-British as free sex. As the oldest industrial capitalist nation in the world, one whose first technological revolution lay well behind it by the time the modernist wave broke over the rest of Europe, Britain was less likely to be swept up in the shock or excitement of the new than France, Italy, Germany, Russia and Scandinavia. It had had plenty of time to assimilate the products of modernity over the course of the centuries. In any case, it had been for some time a largely urban society, and thus with less sense of tension between the old and the new than some of its European neighbours. There was also a sturdy liberal humanist climate, as well as a vigorous current of empiricist thought, both of which proved inhospitable to either modernist or socialist experiment.

Britain was, in fact, a strongly traditionalist civilisation. The cultural influence of its aristocracy long outlived that class's social and economic functions, providing a vital source of authority and stability. In 1848, a year in which there were violent political upheavals elsewhere in Europe, the British working-class movement presented its masters with a set of moderate reformist demands, only to see them haughtily rejected. There was, to be sure, more to the British labour

MODERNISM

movement than a cautious reformism. In 1910, waves of syndicalist strikes embroiled British docks and coalfields. In 1911, troops were despatched throughout the country with orders to fire if necessary on militant workers, and gunboats entered the River Mersey with their guns trained on Liverpool. One year later, the mineworkers launched the greatest strike in British history. Yet if the country was scarcely politically quiescent in the years surrounding the First World War, neither was it in the insurrectionary state into which Russia and some regions of Central Europe had been plunged. France had a far more volatile recent history. The moment of Baudelaire is also that of the 1848 uprising, while the poetry of Arthur Rimbaud belongs in spirit to the outbreak of the Paris Commune of 1871.[39]

The prevailing ethos in Britain was culturally as well as politically conservative. Over the centuries, the nation had developed a vigorous lineage of literary realism from Daniel Defoe to Thomas Hardy, which was to inoculate it to some extent against the modernist adventure. With its milieu of stability and continuity, England proved an attractive refuge for authors like Joseph Conrad who were in flight from more turbulent conditions in their own countries, as well as in later times a remarkable number of Continental historians, aestheticians, sociologists, psychologists and the like, many of whom were in flight from Nazism.[40] It also drew in Americans like James and Eliot, writers in search of a more mannered, traditionalist, densely textured civilisation which might nurture

THE TIME OF MODERNISM

their art. Since these newcomers were for the most part in pursuit of order, tradition and civility, their work tended to affirm the more conservative aspects of British culture. Generally speaking, the cosmopolitan cast of modernism was at odds with both patriotism and provincialism; in the case of exiles in search of a homeland, however, it could also serve to reinforce them.

The region of the United Kingdom most evidently in political turmoil at the time of the modernist project was also one of the most economically stagnant and socially retrograde: Ireland. From the end of the nineteenth century to the aftermath of the First World War, however, Britain's oldest colonial possession was plunged into the maelstrom of revolutionary nationalism, thus fulfilling part of Anderson's recipe for the emergence of modernism. It was also a society in which another of his stipulations – the clash between old and new – was particularly conspicuous. The country had been deindustrialised in the course of the previous century, at a time when it was also crippled by the worst social catastrophe of nineteenth-century Europe, the Great Famine. It was, however, gradually undergoing modernisation, though the heavy industry of the north-east formed a striking contrast with the struggling smallholdings of the west. It is well known that W.B. Yeats lived for a while in one of his own symbols, a much-mythologised Norman tower in County Galway, but less widely bruited that he kept a motor car in a garage beside it. In the shape of the Catholic Church, the British colonial

MODERNISM

presence and the Anglo-Irish Protestant landowning class, the old order was still in force; but it was increasingly under threat from a modern-minded Catholic middle class with nationalist aspirations.

The conditions were ripe, then, for the flourishing of a distinctive Irish modernism, from Yeats, Synge and Joyce to Flann O'Brien and Samuel Beckett. Ireland was also a place accustomed to exile and emigration, which as we shall see later are key features of modernism in general. Few customs have been as central to the country as getting out of it. Joyce and Beckett left their birthplace for Continental Europe, bypassing the imperial metropolis for the cradle of the avant-garde. In doing so, they enacted in voluntary, relatively privileged form the post-Famine experience of millions of their compatriots. The nation was also hospitable to the idea of the artist as rebel and apostate, an image central to modernism as a whole. Its authoritarian Church, colonialist state, nationalist orthodoxies and philistine intellectual climate were fertile breeding grounds for such heretics. Another of Anderson's preconditions for modernism was also to hand, given that the Irish artist had a colonialist 'high' culture to draw upon, but also to react against. There was also an opulent native heritage of scholarship and high art, from the ancient bards to the medieval monasteries and beyond. This included a fabulously rich treasure trove of myth, a literary form on which modernist art habitually draws.

There was thin soil for the growth of a native realism, though a series of nineteenth-century Irish novelists from

THE TIME OF MODERNISM

Maria Edgeworth to George Moore adapted English realist forms to their own ends. The desolate, monotonous quality of everyday life on a spectacularly impoverished island was unlikely to give birth to a Stendhal or Jane Austen. Where Irish writing excelled, however, was in literary modes which realism had largely sidelined: fantasy, Gothic, satire, myth, fable, political rhetoric and the like, most of which lend themselves readily to modernist treatment. It is no surprise that Dracula was a Dubliner, or at least that the novelist who immortalised him hailed from that city. Because the nation's history was so fragmentary and disruptive, its art could embrace the diffuse, dislocated nature of modernism more readily than could the literature of its colonial proprietors. It was able to improvise and innovate, piecing together its cultural and political identity as it went along. Joyce once remarked that it was his freedom from English social and literary convention which lay at the source of his talent, meaning that an Irish colonial was less likely to be hamstrung by the confines of realism than an author from London or Birmingham. It is hard to imagine *Finnegans Wake* emerging from Bognor Regis. As with the Bolshevik venture, it was partly Ireland's 'backwardness', its remoteness from Britain's long history of industrial capitalism and its attendant cultural forms, which allowed Joyce to make his revolutionary leap into the future.

The *Wake* is written in several languages at once, while Synge has been described as the only author who could write in English and Irish simultaneously. If literary modernism

MODERNISM

involves a high degree of linguistic self-consciousness, it is hardly surprising that it should bulk so large in a colony where language had long been a political minefield. The Irish language, already in precipitous decline, was almost dealt its coup de grâce by the Great Famine – a calamity in which it was mostly the poor, who made up the bulk of the Irish speakers, who either died or emigrated. It was the artists, intellectuals and ordinary citizens of the late nineteenth-century Gaelic League who helped to stop the rout of Irish speech and writing. Like a number of modernist literary figures, Wilde, Yeats, Joyce, O'Brien and Beckett were writing in a language which was only ambiguously their own. The artist in exile is typically caught between two or more modes of speech, but for Irish writers this was a common enough dilemma at home. This, then, may be another reason for the prominence of the word in literary modernism: the fact that so many of its authors were disinherited émigrés and expatriates, plunged into the polyglot babble of some Parisian cafe, Viennese studio or Zürich cabaret. A language tends to become more conscious of itself, not least of its own arbitrary nature, when it encounters other forms of speech. It is less likely in such circumstances to mistake itself for the discourse of reality itself. Exile and denaturalisation go together.

Modernist culture turns on a crisis of identity; and since the victims of colonial power can find it hard to say who they are, it is not surprising that such art should thrive in an Ireland which was at the time a region of the British Empire.

THE TIME OF MODERNISM

Modernism is also typically the art of a coterie, one ambiguously suspended between an elite and a vanguard; and Irish modernism found such a group ready to hand in the Anglo-Irish intelligentsia. Yeats, Synge, Augusta Gregory, George Moore, Edward Martyn and a range of other writers were middle-class, aristocratic or would-be aristocratic Protestants, often of partly English descent. As such, they shared in their own peculiar way in the more general crisis of national identity, feeling fully at home neither in Wexford nor in Westminster.

It is from such displaced groups or internal exiles that a good deal of modernist art springs. Uprooted and adrift, strangers on their own soil, the more enlightened of the Anglo-Irish brooded anxiously on the fate of the common people; yet they also felt socially and religiously estranged from these labourers, tenant farmers and tenement dwellers, who had little love for the class they represented. If they were hybrid souls, however, uncertain of where to call home, they also had enough social and cultural authority to lend a voice in the manner of Jonathan Swift to the dire condition of their less well-born compatriots. The social privilege into which they were born could be translated into a cultural elitism typical of modernism. At the same time, the aristocrat's status as semi-outsider could become the spiritual nonconformity of the artistic rebel, or at least find common ground with such figures. It could also forge a pact with the political militancy of the common people, in a lineage of Anglo-Irish nationalist leaders from Wolfe Tone to Charles Stewart Parnell.

MODERNISM

Like some other modernists, these Irish artists looked both forward and backward. Those who were captivated by myth, custom and tradition, like Yeats, Synge and Augusta Gregory, also set themselves up as a cultural vanguard, drawing upon the resources of the past to draft a new future for the nation. We shall see later that modernism is both a cosmopolitan affair and a reversion to the regional and earthbound; and this, too, is evident in the work of some Anglo-Irish modernists, who as progressive, cosmopolitan freethinkers of largely Protestant stock were familiar with the literary scenes of London and Paris, yet who also sought to make amends for their remoteness from the populace by idealising the simple peasant.

Perry Anderson has argued that of all periodising terms, 'modernism' is the most vacuous.[41] It may make sense to describe one's phase of cultural history as Gothic or neoclassical, rococo or Romantic, but what is the point of assigning it a name to which any phase of history can lay claim? Besides, calling yourself modern is rather like forming a club called the Forty-Eighters, carelessly overlooking the fact that next year you will all be forty-nine. To name the new is already to foreshadow its demise. Calling oneself modern is arguably an act of historical hubris, one which involves an oblivion to the future as well as a deletion of the past. Twentieth-century modernism is now a long way behind us – our antiquity, as T.J. Clark wryly puts it,[42] even if some features of it conduct a shadowy afterlife in the form of postmodernism.

THE TIME OF MODERNISM

All historical eras are contemporary with themselves, even if their experience includes much that is archaic or emergent. Yet though every age is modern, not every age lives its experience in these terms; and it is this, presumably, which the term 'modernism' is meant to designate. There is also a difference between being modern and feeling that you ought to be – between 'modern' as descriptive and as prescriptive. It is the latter that marks the advent of modernity, so that to be abreast or ahead of one's times comes to be seen as a virtue in itself. The idea that one's own age lords it over previous, less civilised epochs belongs with this prejudice. Charles Dickens castigated the Victorian England in which he lived, but he also thought it decidedly superior to any previous era of history.

The term 'modernisation' has equally questionable overtones. It means, in effect, a wholesale transformation of the past, one which involves industrialism, technology, secularism, enlightened reason, the mastery of nature, individual autonomy, a war against prejudice, myth and superstition, a faith in freedom and equality and so on. But feudalism transformed antiquity as well, a process to which we do not usually give the name of modernisation. Why should we reserve the word for more recent historical upheavals, and why should it carry an implicitly positive charge? By no means all change is to be commended. 'Modernisation' is one of the most hollow of sociological categories, though whether this is also true of 'modernism' is rather more debatable.

MODERNISM

Let us summarise part of the argument so far. Modernity in general, as opposed to modernism, tends to reject the past, undercut tradition, celebrate the new and look benignly to the future. Yet the modern is nothing if not equivocal. It is also an era which feels itself pregnant with crisis, haunted by apocalypse and alienation and confronted with changes which are as ominous as they are exhilarating.[43] It involves a shift in the very meaning and modality of time: the annihilation of the past, the fetishism of the Now, the elations and anxieties of progress, the imminence for some artists of a brighter future coupled with the sense of a lack of solid ground beneath one's feet.

While some modernist artists embrace this ideology of progress, a good many others are out to dispute it. They affirm the modern in the sense of the original, the innovative and the time of the Now; yet at the same time they anticipate postmodernism in jettisoning the so-called grand narratives (of progress, providence, reason, science, enlightenment and the like) with which modernity is usually associated. For some modernist art, this means that the infinite – a vision of time as rolling endlessly ahead – gives way to the eternal. Time, or history, is no longer linear, uniform, progressive and quantifiable. Instead, it is seen as condensed, elastic, multilayered, diffuse, folded back on itself, crazily accelerated or elided in the name of the eternal moment. It is less 'history' which fascinates such art than the forces unleashed by its suspension. Modernism of this kind represents a rupture in time rather

THE TIME OF MODERNISM

than a specific phase of it. In this sense, it is a period at war with the very idea of periodicity. It is a small token of this indifference to chronology that when an edition of Henry James's novel *The Ambassadors* (1903) managed to reverse the order of two chapters of the narrative, nobody noticed.

2

WORDS AND THINGS

Some modernist art may seek to give history the slip, but attempts to do so are themselves historically significant. They provide an implicit commentary on whatever it is one is fleeing from. For all its suspicion of the temporal, modernism itself, as we have seen, is the product of a major historical crisis, one which includes an upheaval in the realm of ideas. Closely allied with power and self-interest, truth seems increasingly discredited. Its value is now more instrumental than intrinsic. There is also a maladjustment between the mind and its environment. The quicksilver modern mind races ahead of the material world, disdainful of its laws and constraints. The sociologist Georg Simmel claims that 'the essence of modernity as such is psychologism, the experience and interpretation of the world in terms of our inner life . . . the dissolution of fixed contents in the fluid element of the soul, from which all that is substantive is filtered and whose forms are merely forms of

MODERNISM

motion'.[1] Conversely, however, you can see reality itself as in ceaseless flux, a fleeting series of phenomena which the clumsily categorising mind finds almost impossible to capture in its conceptual net. Constant change rocks what were once felt to be stout foundations. God is dead on his feet, or at least is on a life-support machine, traditional bonds have been eroded and community is a dream of the past. What feels like a faceless mass society gives birth to a crisis of subjectivity, as the condition of individuals adrift in the city becomes one of solitude, mutual estrangement or inner collapse. Locked in their private worlds, these people find communication an arduous task. A common reality, not to speak of a sense of totality, is thus harder to come by. Social existence is increasingly specialised and fragmented, so that the workings of the social system become impenetrable to those who inhabit it. It is growing more difficult to map modern society as a whole, or to locate one's place within it. There is no longer an agreed meta-narrative, in the sense of a story which would allow different individuals or cultures to make shared sense of their experience. Yet if each human subject constitutes their own norm, the result is a debilitating relativism.

Some people take refuge from this situation in the depths of the self. Others, far from immersing themselves in an inner life, feel that it has been drained out of them by a dehumanised civilisation. The utilitarian bent of a capitalist culture results, in T.J. Clark's words, in 'a great emptying and sanitising of the imagination'.[2] With industrialism, the world is

WORDS AND THINGS

becoming uglier, and the modernist revolt against realism is among other things a protest against this blight. Yet modernism is also the point at which art, in the tracks of Charles Baudelaire, comes to embrace the squalid or repugnant, which marks a major difference from its Romantic forebears. The monstrous and misshapen are more real, more au courant, than the harmonious and beautiful.

All this takes place at a time when most human beings in the West had never been so well educated and relatively affluent; when many of the common people exercised democratic power, however formally and unevenly; when women were vigorously pursuing their social and political emancipation; when notions of liberty, justice and equality could still be transformative forces; and when everyday life, however harsh and impoverished for the majority, was a good deal more tolerable than it had been for most of their ancestors, not least with the growth of science and technology. We have seen that a number of modernist intellectuals scorned the idea of progress, but this, one imagines, was hardly the view of most of the population. The fact that one could now execute by machine what was once done by hand might seem dehumanising to a small clutch of artists and thinkers, but probably not to those whose labour was alleviated.

If modernity is full of promise and accomplishment, modernism registers the spiritual damage this involves. In Robert Pippin's words, it represents among other things a crisis in modernity's self-confidence.[3] There are concerns that this

MODERNISM

whole emancipatory project has gone disastrously awry, despoiling Nature, inverting freedom into enslavement, draining everyday existence of purpose and value and reducing the individual to a puppet of impersonal forces. The sociologist Max Weber is one of several prophets of doom in this respect. In his view, the reign of humanism and Enlightenment is over, and what we are witnessing in its wake is nothing less than the death of the spirit. For other critics of the modern, excessive rationalism has capsized into madness. Conventional reason has stifled spontaneity, which must now be given free rein in the form of the demonic, Dionysian, mystical, random, libidinal, animal, phantasmal, primitive, excremental, criminal, insane or inhuman. It is the dark shadow cast by a superfluity of enlightenment.

Rather less exotically, the era of modernism was also that of the growth of the reading public. From the closing years of the nineteenth century to about 1920, there was a substantial expansion of the popular press. The reading public in general had grown since the 1830s, but was now doing so at an increasing rate, along with the publishing industry and the number of cheap commercial circulating libraries. Book publication doubled in the first decade of the twentieth century. It was not perhaps until the 1950s that Britain had a majority reading public, but by 1910 there was a majority Sunday-newspaper reading public, and a few years later most of the population were reading daily newspapers as well. It was in the years between 1910 and 1947 – the period, roughly speak-

62

WORDS AND THINGS

ing, of modernism – that a popular press was fully established. The provincial daily press increased in circulation between 1870 and 1890, while the evening press grew significantly from 1880 onwards. By 1900, the recently founded *Daily Mail* was reaching almost a million readers, while the public for daily newspapers in general quadrupled between 1896 to 1914. By the latter date, Sunday newspapers in Britain were selling thirteen million copies.[4]

Modernism and mass culture, then, were twinned at birth. One can add to the growth of newspapers and popular novels the arrival of cinema, radio, the telegraph, the telephone and recorded music. In general, this was not a technological leap forward which literary modernists greeted with acclaim. It is unlikely that Ezra Pound and Virginia Woolf were avid readers of the *Daily Express*. On the contrary, the guardians of high culture tended to see the proliferation of popular reading as a threat to their art, and this distaste for mass literature ranks among the chief characteristics of literary modernism. 'In utilising public means of transport and in making use of information services such as newspapers,' laments the philosopher Martin Heidegger, 'every Other is like the next. This Being-with-one-another dissolves one's own *Dasein* [human existence] completely into the kind of Being of "the Others", in such a way, indeed, that the Others, as distinguishable and explicit, vanish more and more'.[5]

A good many features of modernist writing are reactions to the methods of mass literature. These include its formalism,

MODERNISM

depth, austerity, dissonance, obscurity, impersonality, non-pragmatic nature, reader-unfriendliness, claim to permanent value and verbal self-consciousness. The newspaper, bound fast to the workaday world, conveys information; the modernist work of art, by contrast, is a free-standing object, distrustful of both spontaneous expression and instant communication. The last thing it aims to be is transparent. Reality for mass culture is easily accessible, while for modernism it is dearly won. Some of the Dadaists, who felt that language during the First World War had declined into bombastic military clichés, pasted such slogans satirically into their artworks, along with newspaper headlines and advertising copy.

Yet it is not simply a question of an elitist distaste for pulp fiction and sensational journalism. More fundamentally, the modernists' disdain for the mass reading public reflects an anxiety about the condition of language itself. Language is what binds the literary work to society as a whole; and if the quality of social existence is felt to be cheapened, this is bound to show up in the verbal texture of the artist's work. Since it is language which supplies him with the stuff of his trade, how, under such conditions, is he to write? One deceptively simple answer to this question is: style. Rhetoric is public, but style is personal, a kind of spiritual DNA which cannot be mechanically reproduced. If you come across a poem which is ornate, foppish, precious, full of bravura and outlandish terminology, the author is quite likely to be Wallace Stevens. For the less militantly avant-gardist forms of modernism, the personality

WORDS AND THINGS

of the artist still matters, lurking like a watermark within their inimitable way of writing; while the Romantic cult of genius (later to give way to the postmodernist cult of celebrity) survives in somewhat diminished form. Since a distinctive prose style, bearing the impress of the author's unique identity, is hardly the most eye-catching feature of the *Daily Mirror* or *Murder on the Orient Express*, it may serve to distinguish 'high' art from its popular counterparts.

What makes the difference, in a word, is form, not content. As for the latter, any old subject will do. The point of art is not to reflect its raw materials but to transmute them into something rich and rare, and for this purpose a Parisian sex worker's unmade bed will do just as well as the high altar at Notre Dame. Henry James provocatively declares that the subject of a novel or picture is unimportant. What matters is not the content but the execution. If you can select what subject you like, however, then a fastidious attention to form goes hand in hand with an openness to experiences not generally judged to be fit for art; and both play their part in the scandal of modernism. 'No one in the world ever liked anything so much as Flaubert liked beauty of style,' remarks James,[6] but Flaubert was also notorious for his portrayal of the sordid and seedy, the hackneyed and imbecilic. The artist becomes a secular priest, transubstantiating the profane into the sacred in the ceremony we know as the aesthetic. Art becomes a new religious cult, remote from daily existence, demanding from its practitioners a life of ascetic self-denial and attuned to intimations of immortality. The artist is less a figure awaiting divine inspiration than a craftsman, technician or engineer. For the author Rebecca West, the poet was to be as disciplined and efficient as a stevedore. H.D. was renowned for her punishing work schedule (it is no wonder she disliked her surname 'Doolittle'), along with her devotion to the precise sculpting of language.

Style, for both Flaubert and Joyce, is what transcends content, and thus provides an implicit critique of the everyday banalities in which these writers deal. In this sense, style is itself an irony, at once redeeming and repudiating the world. James called Flaubert's *Sentimental Education* (1869) 'an epic of the usual',[7] and the same might be said of *Ulysses*, *Finnegans Wake* and *The Waste Land*. The Naturalism of authors like Émile Zola, for which very little is too tawdry to fall outside the bounds of art, can be seen as a branch of modernism. What counts in James's view is the intensity of felt life with which reality or experience is rendered, and for this purpose an impatient gesture or shy sideways glance might serve as well as the collapse of a nation state. The novel, he remarks in 'The Future of the Novel' (1900), will take in absolutely anything, a claim which is scarcely borne out by his own socially exclusive brand of fiction. There is a discrepancy between James's generous-spirited sense of what the novel form can accommodate and his genteel distaste for the sociological writings of a Balzac or a Zola. In general, however, the novel is in his view an inherently liberal form, a mode of politics

WORDS AND THINGS

all of its own; and one reason why it needs an integrity of style is that only thus might it draw into unity a vast range of materials that seem to lack all inherent structure.

A caricature of the typical modernist writer, then, would be one who writes a sentence, stares at it intently for an hour or two, puts in a semi-colon, stares at it again for the rest of the morning and then takes it out again just before lunch. Joseph Conrad is a case in point. Marianne Moore remarked that it ought to be work to read something that it was work to write.[8] Whereas popular literature and journalism are examples of mass reproduction, modernist writing is a question of strenuous individual craftsmanship. It is a throwback to an older, more artisanal mode of production, free of the mechanising and commodifying of a faceless popular culture. Instead of mammoth machines churning out miles of newsprint, we have the little press, funded and run by a few devotees of literary distinction. In place of the dehumanised industrial worker there is the sweated labour of one who wrestles not with coal or steel but with the recalcitrant stuff of language, and in doing so produces an object which does not feel alien or anonymous. Rather than confronting an unknowable mass of readers, the writer addresses a civilised coterie who have the leisure and cultivation to appreciate their creations, not simply to consume them in an instant and then grab for more.

Writing, in other words, becomes a form of utopia, however bleak or disenchanted its subject matter. Either it harks back to a more humane, congenial world, or it points forward

MODERNISM

to a social order beyond the mechanising spirit of the present. As Fredric Jameson argues, such art reaps much of its power from 'being a backwater and an archaic holdover within a modernising economy: it glorified, celebrated, and dramatised older forms of individual production which the new mode of production was elsewhere on the point of displacing and blotting out'.[9] If this vein of modernist art gazes back fondly to a world of petty-bourgeois craftsmanship, it also revives in a different form the artistic patronage of an earlier age, when members of the gentry or nobility would bestow commissions on painters, writers, architects and composers. In the case of modernism, the patrons were more likely to be wealthy heiresses or prosperous businessmen with a zeal for poetry and fiction, people who felt honoured to pick up the tab for Pound, Eliot, Joyce, Yeats, Marianne Moore, Wyndham Lewis and other eager recipients of their bounty. Since a number of modernist artists regarded themselves as spiritual aristocrats, they might well have felt secretly superior to the servants of commerce and capital who kept them in shoe leather. One might even be poet and patron at the same time: Gertrude Stein sponsored Picasso, Matisse, Juan Gris, Georges Braque and Francis Picabia.[10]

Art, then, represents a critique of capitalist production simply by what it is, not necessarily by what it says. In this sense, it may even prefigure its own demise. There is no art in the utopian civilisation of William Morris's *News from Nowhere* (1890), since all material production has become creatively

WORDS AND THINGS

fulfilling and the distinction between art and labour has dropped out of sight. It is then easy enough for artists to forget that the industry and mechanisation they abhor have also brought immeasurable benefits to humanity as a whole, not least to writers, painters and composers themselves. From the Romantics onwards, artists have often shown a fine disdain for the material foundations that sustain them. E.M. Forster's novel *Howards End* (1910) is among other things an inquiry into this form of bad faith, even if its solution is simply to be guiltily aware of the fact. The truth that the source of culture is labour is scarcely palatable to those who sing of the autonomy of art, or imagine that it surfaces from some transcendent depth.

With the emergence of the so-called culture industry, 'high' literature becomes an endangered enterprise which feels the need to account for its own existence. With the birth of thrillers and paperback romances, the conviction that the novel can be a form of art now has to be argued for rather than assumed. It is as though the practice of writing has been snatched from your hands and appropriated by a bunch of vulgarians who shamelessly travesty your own most cherished pursuit, but who are a lot more rich and famous than you are as a result. In 'The Art of Fiction' (1888), James argues (unusually for an Anglophone author) for a theory of the novel, which might help to legitimate the form in the face of mass culture. He speaks in 'The Future of the Novel' of being 'in [the] presence of millions for whom taste is but an obscure, confused, immediate instinct', and goes on to fulminate against railway bookstalls.[11]

MODERNISM

He also complains of 'the demoralization, the vulgarization of literature in general, the increasing familiarity of all such methods of communication, the making itself supremely felt, as it were, of the presence of the ladies and children – by whom I mean, in other words, the reader irreflective and uncritical'. It would seem that women, with their penchant for the 'facile flatness' of cheap romantic fiction, must shoulder much of the blame for the corruption of letters.

To do him justice, however, James also insists that 'nothing is more salient in English life today, to fresh eyes, than the revolution taking place in the position and outlook of women', and predicts that it is women authors who will 'smash with final resonance the window all this time most superstitiously closed' in the novel, namely the subject of sexuality.[12] One might add that few modern male authors have put female characters so consistently at the centre of their fiction. Even so, the prospects for fine writing are dire. 'So many ways of producing [a book] have been discovered', James laments, 'that it is by no means the occasional prodigy, for good or for evil, that it was taken for in simpler days, and has therefore suffered a disproportionate discredit.'[13] The rarity value of fine literature is rapidly diminishing, as the practice of reading spawns in all of its 'monstrous multiplications'. The flood of second-rate literature 'at present swells and swells, threatening the whole field of letters, as would often seem, with submersion'.[14] In speaking of 'the loose and thin material that keeps reappearing in forms at once ready-made and sadly the worse for wear', James invites us to compare

WORDS AND THINGS

popular writing to mass-produced clothing.[15] He is also acutely conscious of the negative relation between experimental fiction and a philistine society. 'A community addicted to reflection and fond of ideas', he observes, 'will try experiments with the "story" that will be left untried in a community mainly devoted to travelling and shooting, to pushing trade and playing football.'[16] Football, then, along with females, is another sworn adversary of high art.

It is this sourly dismissive attitude to ordinary life which spurs some modernist art to innovate and experiment. Much of its imaginative flair and spiritual depth are rooted in a fundamental refusal of the familiar. The Russian Formalist doctrine of estrangement, which sees the purpose of art as to cleanse and refresh our perceptions, assumes that everyday life is for the most part boring and banal. Not all modernism, to be sure, harbours this antagonism to routine existence: the Dadaists and Surrealists were fascinated by the detritus of daily life, while the Constructivists, as we shall see, sought to produce useful domestic objects for working people. Even so, it is only with postmodernism that 'high' and 'mass' culture negotiate a truce. The modernist work, by contrast, represents a last-ditch resistance to the commodification of culture. Yet its resentment of the commodity form is ironic, since a commodity is precisely what it is itself. It is thus a self-divided phenomenon, and part of its integrity consists in acknowledging its own bad faith in this respect. It must confess its complicity with the very system it seeks to repel.

MODERNISM

One way in which the modernist artwork can resist the shame of commodification is by making itself hard to consume. Creme caramel slips down easily, but Pound's *Cantos* does not. Instead, the reader is forced into a labour of interpretation, becoming a co-author of the work along with the artist. Nietzsche was a champion of what he called 'slow reading', while James Joyce once remarked, no doubt tongue in cheek, that he wanted the reader to spend as long reading *Finnegans Wake* as he took to write it. In an anticipation of what would later be known as reception theory, Dorothy Richardson insisted that readers were not passive recipients but active co-creators of the work. As the Russian Formalist Viktor Shklovsky remarks of everyday phenomena:

> The thing rushes past us, pre-packed as it were; we know that it is there by the space it takes up, but we see only its surface. This kind of perception shrivels a thing up, first of all in the way we perceive it, but later this affects the way we handle it too . . . Life goes to waste as it is turned into nothingness. Automatisation corrodes things, clothing, furniture, one's wife and one's fear of war . . . And so that a sense of life may be restored, that things may be felt, there exists what we call art.[17]

It is heartening to learn that Shklovsky's interest in poetic devices led him to conclude that his wife was not an automaton. 'Poetry', writes the Imagist T.E. Hulme in a similar vein, 'always

WORDS AND THINGS

endeavours to arrest you, and to make you continuously see a physical thing, to prevent you gliding through an abstract process.'[18] It is an affront to the anaemic prose of the technocrats and administrators, as well as to the dizzying stampede of city life.

Obscurity is a constitutive feature of some modernist art, not simply a sign of the limited understanding of its audience. The writer doesn't want to be understood, remarks Jean-Paul Sartre in *What Is Literature?* (1948). Difficulty is now a hallmark of high culture, distinguishing the connoisseur from the common reader. Among other things, it is a protest against what modernism regards as the spurious transparency of the language of science, commerce, politics, advertising and everyday existence. Given the speed and evanescence of modern life, people are in danger of losing their capacity for genuine experience, as fragments of the world bombard them from all angles but refuse to sediment in the depths of their psyches. If this capacity fails, there is no future for the artist, at least of a traditional kind. The death of experience prefigures the end of art.

So it is that the literary text must thicken its language, dislocate its syntax and scramble its narrative in order to force its readers into the kind of attentiveness which they would be unlikely to lavish on a bus ticket. We are made to re-create the work from moment to moment, pay dearly for our enjoyment of it, savour language in the very process of its occurrence. The reader of an author like Gerard Manley Hopkins, having

MODERNISM

wrestled for a while with his sinewy, muscular verse, looks forward to nothing more than a few relaxing hours in bed. Gertrude Stein's experiments in prose and poetry, considered by most of her contemporaries to be either risible or outrageous, involve deviant syntax, incessant repetition, the abandonment of plot, punctuation and linear progression and the disruption of conventional word order. There are sentences in her work which reveal a deep reluctance to stop, as well as a carefully cultivated awkwardness or naivety of tone and style. A passage from *The Making of Americans* (1925) reads: 'These have it in them then to have when they have quick reaction in them that is not a stirring from the depths of them these have it very often than this in them is a violent attacking . . .'

In the first volume of *Capital* (1867), Karl Marx portrays the commodity as an abstract phenomenon, however tangible it may seem, since its value is determined not by its material qualities but by its ability to exchange with another commodity embodying the same amount of labour-power. And since this can be any object at all, commodities are purely formal entities, largely indifferent to the sensuous and specific. In this sense, they are the opposite of poetry. From Romanticism to modernism, the sensory nature of the literary work, its vigilance to the feel and flavour of things, provides an implicit critique of the abstract social order in which it is forced to survive. The poem can try to avoid commodity status by becoming a palpable object, drawing attention to its own intricate materiality. It becomes an autonomous thing like an urn,

WORDS AND THINGS

gem or icon, closed off from its social context and unique in its identity. In this sense, it is everything that the commodity is not. Yet the irony is that as a material thing endowed with a mysterious power, the work also comes to resemble a kind of fetish; and fetishism, at least in Marx's view, is a notable feature of the commodity form. The autonomous work of art is the commodity as fetish resisting the commodity as abstract exchange. In this sense, too, it is divided against itself.

Faced with this dilemma, the work of art may try to remain open to the world rather than insulating itself from it. It may blur the boundaries between itself and reality, presenting itself as unfinished, open-ended, incapable of being totalised. The work becomes a non-thing rather than a self-contained object. Hence the interest of some avant-gardists in art as gesture, happening, situation, performance, manifestation – processes which consume themselves before you can get to consume them yourself. Paint a moustache on the Mona Lisa or wrap the Bank of England in cellophane. Let Microsoft try hanging *that* in the lobby of its headquarters.

A play, Bertolt Brecht remarks, must give the audience a sense that there is always more production still possible.[19] In highlighting the arbitrariness of its own limits, it can hint at unspoken meanings, unrealised possibilities, alternative narratives. The poem, likewise, becomes a web of suggestions and allusions without clearly etched frontiers, a work which no single reading can exhaust. It is a new text each time one returns to it. Baudelaire praises poetry which seems dashed off

MODERNISM

and rough at the edges, lacking the polish of the classical arte-fact. A poem is never completed, only abandoned, insists the poet and aesthetician Paul Valéry. Dorothy Richardson, suspi-cious of closure, leaves her mammoth novel *Pilgrimage* open-ended. There are no set limits to language, since one sign implicates another, and that another. 'Experience', writes Henry James in a memorable image, 'is never limited, and is never complete; it is an immense sensibility, a kind of huge spider-web of the finest silken threads suspended in the cham-ber of consciousness, and catching every air-borne particle in its tissue.'[20] All literary form, then, is a kind of cheating – a shaping and selecting of experiences which are in reality boundless. It follows that the most authentic work of art is one which acknowledges its own artifice in this respect. If re-alism is akin to dyeing your hair so that its colour looks natu-ral, modernism and postmodernism are like dyeing it deep purple or bright orange. Nobody imagines that you looked like that at the age of seven.

If the language of the literary work is becoming opaque, it is also because the world it represents is growing increasingly difficult to decipher. A citizen of medieval Europe would no doubt have found it hard to imagine a civilisation like our own, in which most of us have no idea how some of our most familiar tools and contrivances actually work. It is thus that a form of Romantic socialism dreams of a future social order which would be entirely transparent to itself. In the mean-time, however, modern experience appears so complex and

WORDS AND THINGS

fragmented that it threatens to elude all determinate sense. Or if not that, then it seems to possess such a luminous, quasi-mystical presence that language is struck hollow, as words fall from one's lips like so many empty husks.

Such is the experience of Lord Chandos in Hugo von Hofmannsthal's 'The Chandos Letter' (1902), whose ability to make conceptual sense of reality is gradually falling apart, afflicted as he is by a kind of spiritual aphasia:

> I have completely lost the ability to think or speak coherently about anything at all ... Rather, the abstract words which the tongue must enlist as a matter of course in order to bring out an opinion disintegrated in my mouth like rotten mushrooms. It happened to me that, when I wanted to scold my four-year-old daughter Katharina Pompilia ... the ideas flowing into my mouth suddenly took on such iridescent hues and merge into each other to such a degree that I had to make an effort to sputter to the end of my sentence, as if I had fallen in ... Everything came to pieces, the pieces broke into more pieces, and nothing could be encompassed by one idea. Isolated words swam about me; they turned into eyes which stared at me and into which I had to stare back, dizzying whirlpools which spun around and around and led into the void.[21]

Chandos, one might claim, is suffering from a severe attack of modernism. Indeed, the letter is a key document of the

MODERNISM

movement. In Malcolm Bull's words, 'Chandos's terrifying experience enacts within the compass of a single life the entire social transformation described by modernity.'[22] Language is treacherous stuff, no longer providing any assured access to reality. Chandos continues to experience things with almost psychedelic intensity: 'A watering can, a harrow left in a field, a dog in the sun, a shabby churchyard, a cripple, a small farmhouse – any of these can become the vessel of my revelation.'[23] But they do not reveal the truth of themselves in the enervated medium of words, which Chandos has given up as a bad job. It is as though their meaning is as much part of their physical being as their shape and colour, so that it cannot pass from the thing to the sign.

Like a Symbolist poet, Chandos senses with wordless rapture the presence of infinity in everything he encounters; but to articulate this depth he would need a language beyond language – 'not Latin or English, or Italian, or Spanish, but a language of which I know not one word, a language in which mute things speak to me and in which I will perhaps have something to say for myself some day when I am dead and standing before an unknown judge'.[24] It would be, so to speak, the language of beings themselves, renouncing their customary muteness to give voice to their secret essences. Any less immanent form of discourse is bound to thrust the world at arm's length in the act of trying to formulate it, and so is likely to falsify it. Words and things have come unstuck from one other: Fredric Jameson speaks of a 'dissociation of the existent and the meaningful' in modernist art, or 'the contradiction

78

WORDS AND THINGS

between the contingency of physical objects and the demand for an impossible meaning'.[25] One thinks of T.S. Eliot's line in *Four Quartets*, 'We had the experience, but missed the meaning', which many a baffled reader has felt to be true of Eliot's own work – not least of his drama, where the action seems to move at one level and the significance at another. One consequence of this divorce of sign and object, as we shall see in a moment, is that if words can no longer mediate things, they can always compensate for this deficiency by becoming things in their own right.

The world has not lost its significance in Chandos's eyes. On the contrary, it is so surcharged with sense as to be ineffable. But it no longer discloses any overall structure or design. It is impossible to sort things into the more and less important. 'To me', Chandos writes, 'there was no difference between drinking warm foaming milk which a tousled rustic at my hunting lodge had squeezed into a wooden bucket from the udder of a fine, mild-eyed cow, and drinking in sweet and frothy spiritual nourishment from an old book as I sat in the window seat of my study.'[26] 'Everything seems to mean something,' he adds with a disturbingly paranoid touch, 'everything that exists . . . as if my body consisted entirely of coded messages revealing everything to me.'[27] It is just that his decoding mechanisms have disastrously failed. There is no longer any inherent order in the world – though it is not clear how we could peer beyond our concepts (which lend some coherence to reality) to know that what lies beyond them is chaos. Language may foist a

MODERNISM

structure on the world, however gratuitously; yet speech, too, is disintegrating fast, so that Chandos is deprived of even this meagre consolation.

It is no great step, then, from his 'everything seems to mean something' to the claim that 'everything exists, nothing has value', a proposition from E.M. Forster's novel *A Passage to India*. It is through language that we order, classify and discriminate, and to lose this capability is to confront a world in which hierarchies have collapsed and nothing is more precious or sense-bearing than anything else. A mollusc may have as much claim on one's attention as a famished child. If this is so, then it is hard to see how one can shape a poem or construct a narrative, at least in the conventional sense. Moreover, since things are bound intimately together, every object or experience becomes an intimation of everything else, so that nothing has any natural stopping point. As a result, reality is sprawling and shapeless, and form becomes pure fiction. There can be no structures, relations or comparisons. To rank is to falsify. As with the commodity form, everything is reduced to the same dead level, as Chandos finds himself incapable of advancing an opinion on even the most mundane of subjects, let alone on more exalted metaphysical matters. Perhaps those postmodern thinkers for whom all hierarchy is pernicious might care to think again.

Chandos's loss of language is also a loss of certainty. Truth is not a feature of reality but of what we assert about reality, and one cannot frame such assertions if words taste like rotten

WORDS AND THINGS

mushrooms in one's mouth. For some modernists, as we shall see later, words have become blunted and banal, and so are no fit medium of truth. At the same time, the world has splintered into a host of colliding perspectives, as many perhaps as there are individual human subjects, and there is no meta-language in which one might judge which of them is more valid than others.

A strikingly similar condition to Chandos's afflicts the narrator of W.G. Sebald's novel *Austerlitz* (2001). Meaning disintegrates into disconnected marks, rather as time for some modernist thinkers lapses into a series of discrete moments. Interpretation is a discursive affair, as one unpacks the meaning of an utterance from moment to moment; and if time itself is now gradually imploding, it is not surprising that sense-making should crumble along with it. This, ironically, is a condition which Gertrude Stein, far from lamenting à la Chandos, is actually seeking to attain. She wants to free words from meanings, 'to like the feeling of words doing as they want to do and as they have to do' without the bondage of everyday sense.[28]

Obscurity, ambiguity and indeterminacy are among the typical features of modernist writing. In T.S. Eliot's poem 'A Cooking Egg' (1917), the narrator recalls eating what he calls 'the penny world' behind a screen with someone called Pipit, while 'red-eyed scavengers are creeping / From Kentish Town and Golder's Green'. What is a penny world? Some kind of cake or sweet, perhaps? Is there a touch of Proustian nostalgia

MODERNISM

here, as the narrator recalls a cherished childhood experience which has vanished as completely as the penny world itself disappeared down his digestive tract? 'Penny world' sounds as though it means something, but maybe it is just a verbal contrivance. Perhaps there is no object in the world to correspond to the words. Anyway, why are Pipit and the narrator eating it behind a screen? Is this a private moment of guilty self-indulgence? Perhaps Pipit is or was the narrator's nursemaid or governess (another verse informs us that the character is female), though the name 'Pipit' doesn't sound much like a governess, more like one of Evelyn Waugh's Bright Young Things.

Who are the red-eyed scavengers, and why are these faintly nightmarish creatures creeping across north-west London? Red-eyed scavengers are scavengers with red eyes; but though we know what the individual words mean, we don't know what 'red-eyed scavengers' means, any more than we do 'penny world'. You can only understand signs in context, and no context is provided. Perhaps these creatures, too, exist purely at the level of the signifier. Like a good deal in Eliot's poetry, the words look as though they have a referent (some object in the real world which they denote), but this may be an illusion. It is as though the words of the poem point not outward to some independent reality but inward to each other; and the effect of this is to create a dense mesh of resonances and cross-currents which *is* their meaning. Because we cannot give a definitive sense to the phrase 'red-eyed scavengers', it becomes a little text all in itself, an echo chamber of dim allusions and ominous

WORDS AND THINGS

associations. What looks denotative is in fact connotative: the point is not to indicate an actual phenomenon but to generate an emotional climate, rather as Eliot's magnificent poem 'Gerontion' (1920) looks at one point as though it is portraying certain individual characters but is actually creating an atmosphere of the exotic, overbred, cosmopolitan and slightly spooky.

'Red-eyed scavengers' evokes vague but unsettling notions of the savage and predatory. One might contrast the creatures in this respect with Yeats's rough beast in his poem 'The Second Coming' (1919), another image of impending barbarism but one which is clearly delineated rather than menacingly suggestive. Yeats's beast shuffles and slouches, rather as Eliot's scavengers creep, and this is creepy because the verbs suggest some stealthy, inexorable, unstoppable process, like something in a bad dream. (Yeats's 'slouch', however, may also have class connotations: slouching, as opposed to strutting or striding, is what the 'lower orders' are supposed to do).

Some scholars have suggested that Yeats's rough beast has a relation to Bolshevism. 'The Second Coming' appeared in a volume of 1921, four years after the Russian insurrection, while Eliot's piece appeared only three years after it. To point out that like the scavengers' eyes the colour of revolutionary socialism is red would be a distasteful example of vulgar Marxism, which is why this study will refrain from doing so. Nor would one want to make too much of the fact that Karl Marx once lived in Kentish Town.

MODERNISM

What may indeed be worth noting, however, is that in a period of labour militancy the scavengers are creeping from a largely working-class area of London, as Kentish Town was in that period, as well as from a traditionally Jewish neighbourhood, Golders Green. Eliot harboured some anti-Semitic sentiments at the time, and was probably not well acquainted with Golders Green, which may be one reason why he gets the name wrong ('Golder's' instead of 'Golders'). It is interesting that the poem becomes determinate in its references at this point, unlike its effort elsewhere to hold us at the level of the signifier. It wants us to know something of the social context of the forces which the scavengers represent, while at the same time keeping the danger they pose ill-defined and thus all the more menacing.

Yeats is a symbolic poet, in the straightforward sense that he uses symbols, but Eliot is a Symbol*ist* writer, which is a different affair. In Yeats's case, there is generally a clear distinction between symbol and thing, or sign and referent. In fact, it is a relationship to which he occasionally draws our attention in a series of rather grand gestures: 'I declare this tower my tower' . . . 'another emblem there!' . . . What's water but the generated soul?' . . . 'Players and painted stage took all my love, / And not those things that they were emblems of.' With a Symbolist poet like Mallarmé or Eliot, however, it is harder to distinguish between language and reality. Language in Eliot is rammed up so closely against sensory content that there is no real space between the two. This means among other things that the poem is

WORDS AND THINGS

unable to pass an explicit judgement on what it speaks of, as Yeats's writing frequently does. Instead, its judgements tend to be implicit and insinuated. Yet the spatial metaphor is misleading, since there is in fact no distance between language and reality, and no intimacy between them either.

Wallace Stevens parodies this Symbolist style of writing in the first two lines of his poem 'Bantams in Pine-Woods' (1922): 'Chieftain Iffucan of Azcan in caftan / Of tan with henna hackles, halt!' Through assonance, rhythm and alliteration, the words are more intent on setting up relations with each other than on what they denote, as the signifier flamboyantly displaces attention from the signified. Ridiculously clogged and cluttered, the poem makes it absurdly obvious that the chieftain to which it purports to refer is no more than a gaudy riot of sound. Its elaborate artifice is ironically at odds with the stereotype of tribal peoples as simple and natural.

What is the point of such exhibitionism? To answer this question, we must take a brief detour through the concept of everyday life. Every historical age has such a thing, of course, in the sense of the routine experience of the common people; but it is only in the modern age that this sphere is raised to the status of a philosophical concept, and philosophies of the everyday begin to stage their appearance.[29] Run-of-the-mill features of daily life become portentous metaphysical ideas: boredom or 'mood' for Martin Heidegger, nausea for Jean-Paul Sartre, the way we experience our bodies for some other phenomenological thinkers. Sartre is said to have turned pale

85

MODERNISM

with excitement when the philosopher Maurice Merleau-Ponty arrived hot-foot with the news that you could make philosophy out of the ashtray. The semiotician Roland Barthes decodes wrestling matches and restaurant menus, while Mikhail Bakhtin writes learned discourses on laughter. Gershom Scholem remarks that 'a philosophy which does not include the possibility of sooth-saying from *coffee grounds* cannot be a true philosophy'.[30] All this had been foreshadowed by Friedrich Nietzsche, who asked why no philosopher had ever spoken with reverence of the human nose.

All the same, there is a powerful feeling among modernist writers that daily existence in an urban, industrialised world has become barren, and that human experience has been cheapened and diminished. If this is so, you can burrow beneath the everyday to some deeper level of myth and archetype. Alternatively, you can soar above it to some loftier spiritual realm. There are also those who retreat from a degraded reality into the more profitable depths of the self. 'We speak not to be understood but to our inner selves,' comments the avant-garde dramatist Antonin Artaud.[31] Yet inner and outer worlds are not always to be strictly opposed. Dorothy Richardson's *Pilgrimage* is a study in the 'deep' subjectivity of its protagonist, Miriam Henderson; yet because the subject in question is a woman, and thus part of an oppressed sector of society, this exploration of inwardness is bound to be political as well. Ironically, it is by turning to the self that one can engage most effectively with social and political questions. At

WORDS AND THINGS

the same time, *Pilgrimage* combines the inner investigations of a Woolf with the fastidiously detailed social landscape of a Joyce, which is one reason why the term used of it by one critic – 'stream of consciousness' – is peculiarly inept. It is equally misleading as an account of the style of Proust and Joyce. Proust's gargantuan novel contains some of the most wickedly satirical accounts of French high society ever written, not simply adventures in internal space.

You can also stylise the hackneyed or nondescript so as to reap some aesthetic value from it, in the manner of Flaubert and Joyce. Perhaps some fragments of a drably prosaic world might still be salvaged for art. We have seen already that the Dadaists and Surrealists were fascinated by the flotsam and jetsam of everyday culture. So, too, were the Cubists. The Surrealists looked for the magical in the commonplace, while even the Olympian Eliot had a faintly patronising fondness for jazz and music hall. By and large, however, the modernist attitude to the everyday is chillingly negative. It is mostly a question of *ennui*, a Baudelarian term for which 'boredom' is too feeble a translation. Day-to-day experience is no longer fit for artistic purpose, and so must be purified, ironised, intensified or pitched into crisis.

The work of Samuel Beckett is intriguing in this respect, since it combines a typically modernist sense of extremity with an unflinching focus on the commonplace. If its emotional milieu is one of spiritual desolation, it also steers clear of any too solemn preoccupation with spiritual depth, not least in its

MODERNISM

flatness and stringent economy. Extremity is now a routine affair, as it was for Beckett himself in his years of hunger and hardship during the Nazi occupation of France. Unlike some of his modernist colleagues, he is not in the least interested in heightened states of consciousness – in mysticism, the occult, sado-masochism or the emancipatory effects of hashish. On the contrary, he is the most everyday of extremists.

Modernism represents a crisis of language in a civilisation that tends to treat the stuff in largely utilitarian ways. Among other things, it is a response to the fate of discourse in a commercial, bureaucratised society. The narrator of Beckett's *Malone Dies* (1951/6) speaks up for language in a notably backhanded way, remarking that 'there is no use indicting words, they are no shoddier than what they peddle'. If language is sullied, the blame must fall on the society to which it belongs. Like many aspects of modernism, this situation is scarcely new. Goethe and Schiller were complaining toward the end of the eighteenth century that language was being sapped and degutted. How is one to convey truth and beauty when literature is besieged on all sides by purely technical or pragmatic forms of speech? Later critics asked what happens to writing in an era of banner headlines, swollen political rhetoric, calculative reason and cynically manipulative advertising. How is it to avoid being polluted by the bloodless prose of science and technology? In reciting poems composed of pure sound, the Dadaist Hugo Ball declares that 'in these phonetic power must return to the innermost alchemy of the

WORDS AND THINGS

word . . . we totally renounce the language that journalism has abused'.[32] The play of the signifier was his vengeance on the popular press. His pre-Dadaist life, however, was in turn to exact its revenge on him. In one performance of liturgical chanting, he found himself transported back to his Catholic childhood and had to be carried off the stage bathed in sweat. Soon after, he abandoned Dada to devote himself to religious studies. God moves in a mysterious way.

One answer to the question of how writing can survive a world of degenerate speech and adulterated experience is for literature to seize on the stuff of everyday language and try to redeem it. A good deal of literary modernism is marked by a certain verbal exuberance, but this does not spring from any very profound faith in the word. On the contrary, modernist authors are for the most part deeply distrustful of language, at least in its common-or-garden state. (James Joyce, who believed that language could represent anything at all, is a rare exception.) Words have become grubby and shop-soiled, worn thin like old coins by myriad social exchanges, and must be cleansed or freshly minted if they are to become once more a suitable medium for artistic expression. They must be twisted or compressed, purified or dislocated, subjected to a systematic violence which will force them into yielding up whatever fragments of truth still lurk within them.

This is another modernist doctrine with a lengthy history. 'I can yield you [no reason] without words,' remarks the Fool in Shakespeare's *Twelfth Night*, 'and words are grown so false I

MODERNISM

am loath to prove reason with them.' Words, he complains, 'are very rascals since bonds disgrac'd them', meaning by bonds commercial contracts. It is largely from the modernist era that we inherit a number of high-minded clichés about the deficiencies of discourse: 'if I could tell you I would let you know', 'words are just so inadequate', 'all the most precious truths lie too deep for expression' and the like. At the risk of stating the obvious, one might point out that statements like 'words are utterly empty' are self-refuting. What would be the point of saying so if it were true?

Another reason for this inarticulacy is the sheer complexity of experience in the modern age, which language has to struggle to record. The world would seem to be too brute, fast-moving, atomised, opaque and fantasy-ridden to be easily represented. As we have seen, it is a modernist commonplace that reality is mercurial, quick-moving stuff, whereas language and the intellect are laborious devices continually outstripped by it. For the modernist philosopher Henri Bergson's *Creative Evolution* (1907), there are no things, only processes. Nouns are simply reified verbs. What we need are concepts fluid enough to capture the sinuous inner life of things. The world itself, so to speak, is becoming steadily less realist, so that even the language of science finds itself faltering. For the physicist Werner Heisenberg, we cannot speak of the reality revealed by nuclear physics with any exactitude. In any case, mind is simply an accidental spin-off of evolution, and as such is inherently alienated from its material surroundings. The gap

WORDS AND THINGS

between word and thing signifies a rift between consciousness and reality.

One needs, then, a language supple and delicate enough to capture the momentary flow and recoil of experience, as well as the flux of objective reality. This is particularly vital in a civilisation which has pressed individualism to the point where everyone's inner life appears locked inside their bodies. The more your experience is uniquely your own, and thus supremely precious, the harder it is to convey it, and so to confirm its reality. Inner and outer worlds split apart. 'The self-confident word', remarks Arnheim in Robert Musil's novel *The Man Without Qualities* (1930–43), 'gives an arbitrary and poverty-stricken form to the invisible motions of our inner being.' This is already a problem for Charles Dickens, in whose novels communication is often a random interlocking of monologues rather than anything one might call a genuine dialogue. Apart from figures like Oliver Twist, who despite being brought up in a workhouse speaks impeccable standard English, most of Dickens's characters have their trademark mode of speech – quickfire delivery, verbose ramblings, wheedling whine, exaggerated lisp, pretentious cant – which obstructs communication rather than enabling it. Idiosyncrasies which are amusing in Dickens's earlier fiction, however, may take on a more ominous tone in his later work. We are now in a world which seems populated by a set of self-enclosed monads whose chance encounters are more a matter of collision than conversation. The Russian film director Sergei

MODERNISM

Eisenstein acknowledged the influence of this Dickensian vision on the disjunctive techniques of early cinema, not least on his own work.[33]

Perhaps one can come up with a new language suitable for modern circumstances. Virginia Woolf writes of Dorothy Richardson that she has invented a peculiarly feminine style of prose which is 'of a more elastic fibre than the old, capable of stretching to the extreme, of suspending the frailest particles, of enveloping the vaguest shapes'.[34] The notoriously cobwebby style of the late Henry James is one attempt to hold the intricacies of everyday thought and feeling together by a heroic effort of style, syntax and scintillating intelligence:

> That itself indeed, for our restless friend, became by the end of a week the very principle of reaction: so that he woke up one morning with such a sense of having played a part as he needed self-respect to gainsay. He hadn't in the least stated at Lancaster Gate that, as a haunted man – a man haunted with a memory – he was harmless; but the degree to which Mrs Lowder accepted, admired and explained his new aspect laid upon him practically the weight of a declaration. What he hadn't in the least stated her own manner was perpetually stating; it was as haunted and harmless that she was constantly putting him down. There offered itself however to his purpose such an element of plain honesty, and he had embraced, by the time he dressed, his proper corrective.[35]

WORDS AND THINGS

There are far more impenetrable passages than this in James's later fiction. Marcel Proust's fluent, supremely effortless sentences, which can unfurl over half a page or more, are similar triumphs of syntax, as a labyrinth of impeccably well-ordered clauses and sub-clauses gathers the slightest flickers and tremors of consciousness into a single, virtuoso performance. Virginia Woolf achieves something of the same effect, shorn of James's excessive fastidiousness:

> . . . so that the monotonous fall of the waves on the beach, which for the most part beat a measured and soothing tattoo to her thoughts and seemed consolingly to repeat over and over again as she sat with the children the words of some old cradle song, murmured by nature, 'I am guarding you – I am your support', but at other times suddenly and unexpectedly, especially when her mind raised itself slightly from the task actually in hand, had no such kindly meaning, but like a ghostly roll of drums remorselessly beat the measure of life, made one think of the destruction of the island and its engulfment in the sea, and warned her whose day had slipped past in one quick doing after another that it was all ephemeral as a rainbow.[36]

The passage flows with the unforced, accumulative power of the waves themselves, in contrast to James's more self-conscious prose; yet this life-giving abundance is also a ceaseless decaying and evanescing, as each of Woolf's clauses gives

MODERNISM

way to another in a syntactical overflow in which, as with the ocean, nothing stays still for a moment.

The classical realist novel presumes the existence of a common language, one which links it to its readers and links readers to one another. Given the host of specialist idioms of the modern age – what one might call the accelerating division of linguistic labour – this kind of lingua franca is less easy to come by. Joyce's *Ulysses* is written in a medley of different styles, with no voiceover or meta-language to draw them coherently together or rank them in significant order. 'What is Joyce's style in *Ulysses*?' is an unanswerable question. Mallarmé protests that 'languages are imperfect because multiple; the supreme language is missing . . . without the sound of the immortal Word, the diversity of languages on earth means that no one can utter words which would bear the miraculous stamp of Truth Herself incarnate'.[37] It is a high modernist lamentation very far from postmodern celebrations of diversity. An aesthetic which had served the European middle classes superbly well in its day (classical realism) is nearing its point of breakdown – partly because modern experience seems both too nuanced and too abstruse to be adequately represented, and partly because the means of registering it have become deeply problematic. Modernism is thus among other things a crisis of representation, as familiar forms of language no longer appear to map on to the changed conditions of modern life.[38] Jacques Rancière writes that 'this [modernist] paradigm determines artistic modernity as the break of every kind of art

94

WORDS AND THINGS

with the enslavement of representation'.[39] One can read Dorothy Richardson's *Pilgrimage* as a reflection on the false representation of women in patriarchal society, or indeed on the impossibility of representing them at all.

What escapes representation above all is the human subject, which is no kind of substance or entity and thus threatens to slip through the net of language. It is an impenetrable enigma on which the whole world turns. We cannot grasp ourselves as subjects, so the theory runs, since we could do so only from within the distortions of subjectivity itself; or because we would need to be standing at some impossible Archimedean point outside ourselves; or because we would instantly turn ourselves into knowable objects and thus cease to be subjects at all. The very consciousness which posits reality in the first place falls outside reality's frame of reference, and so cannot be figured there. The mind is not 'in' the world at all. It is a problem familiar enough to the Romantics and German Idealists, and thus yet another aspect of modernism which is unoriginal. The name given by some of these thinkers to the unrepresentable was the sublime, which is by no means always an agreeable place to be; and one way of seeing modernism is as a shift from beauty (for which Victorian poets continue to strive) to sublimity.

If language is untrustworthy and reality undecipherable, then perhaps one might break through to the truth only by wreaking a certain violence upon them both. One might call this the Room 101 syndrome, after George Orwell's novel

MODERNISM

Nineteen Eighty-Four (1949), in which a character is removed from his customary environment and pushed to his outer limit, feeling meaning and morality falling from him like so many useless rags. It is at this moment of spiritual crisis that the truth will finally stand naked before him. It is a commonplace of the modernist philosophy of existentialism, and might be called the torture chamber theory of truth. Routine social existence is false and shallow, and only at moments of epiphany or unbearable pressure will the truth flare out. You must penetrate the brittle surface to delve to the inner depth.

Much the same is true of language, which must be shaken and stirred if it is to yield up any genuine meaning. Hardly anyone in the eighteenth century or the Victorian period shared these convictions, but modernism tends to regard the fragility of language, the elusiveness of truth and the opaqueness of reality as universal axioms. There is something extremist about its vision, which may be another reason why it never took off as vigorously in stereotypically middle-of-the-road Britain as it did in Continental Europe. In any case, the Room 101 syndrome is surely suspect: why should what is said at moments of terror or despair be taken for the truth? Orwell's protagonist betrays his lover when a bunch of the animals he fears most – rats – threaten to chew through his cheek, and most other people, including the lover, would surely do the same.

This whole aesthetic is also an implicit politics. It assumes that the everyday world is inauthentic, which is truer of show-

WORDS AND THINGS

business than it is of health centres or kindergartens. The typical modernist view of daily existence is aloofly indiscriminate, lumping together mindless consumerism with teaching the deaf or patching up injured donkeys. The vision of the ordinary as alienated is itself alienated. It reflects the conditions of an isolated, inward-looking intelligentsia, from whose exalted vantage point the whole world appears lacklustre. Yet everyday life in the modernist period was shaken by a whole series of tumultuous political events involving ordinary people, which promised to transform the world rather more effectively than art. *The Waste Land* imagines crowds of people walking pointlessly round in a ring; but this innocuous activity is one which the British government of the time, fearful as it was of popular insurrection, might well have welcomed.

If language is soiled and tarnished, what other strategies can the modernists adopt to infuse it with fresh life? You can strike a defeatist posture and try to use as little of the stuff as you can. T.S. Eliot was of the view that most poets should write as little as possible. Perhaps the ideal poem would be a blank page; but although there can be no literary work without words, you can make those words frugal and tight-lipped, as in the work of Beckett or Hemingway, H.D., William Carlos Williams, Albert Camus, Paul Celan or Alain Robbe-Grillet, avoiding all excess and ornamentation. It is what Roland Barthes calls 'writing degree zero' in his study of that title. If language is a medium of deception and bad faith, then the

MODERNISM

more ruthlessly you whittle it down the less likely it is to double-cross you. The less you say, the less you can dupe and manipulate. Once this parsimony itself becomes obtrusive – becomes, as with Camus or Hemingway, a style in itself – we have shifted from realism to modernism.

You can also slim down the content. 'The finest works are those which contain the least matter,' writes Gustave Flaubert.[40] Henry James speaks in an essay on Flaubert of 'his immense ado about nothing'. Pound and his fellow Imagists demand a poetry which treats concrete particulars with luminous clarity and a minimum of verbal mediation. Vague Romantic generalities are to be junked. You can press the issue even further by reducing human communication to an inarticulate stutter. There is the Expressionist cry of anguish, bellow of rebellion or blood-curdling shriek, as language is hacked down to a howl of rage. Or you can replace words with non-verbal sounds: one Italian Futurist declares that 'we derive far more pleasure from ideally combining the noises of trams, internal combustion engines, carriages and noisy crowds than from rehearsing, for example, "The Eroica" or the "Pastoral"'.[41]

In the so-called Theatre of Cruelty of Antonin Artaud, script is sacrificed to sound, image and physical motion. The only sure mode of communication is the body. In Jacques Derrida's view, such drama represents 'the shout that the artic-ulations of language and logic have not yet entirely frozen', a stage 'whose clamour has not yet been pacified into words'.[42] Language, in a word, gentrifies reality. You must therefore

WORDS AND THINGS

pare away everything about it that seems extraneous, like the Imagists with their compact nuggets of verse, or like the Russian Suprematist painters' stripping away of shape and colour so that the truth of the void beneath them might be laid bare. H.D. and Marianne Moore both aim for a scrupulous exactitude of poetic diction, while Gertrude Stein believed that the vitality of the English language lay in the simplicity of its grammar.[43]

Language, writes Walter Benjamin of the Surrealists, 'only seemed itself where sound and image, image and sound interpenetrated with automatic precision and such felicity that no chink was left for the penny-in-the-slot called "meaning" '.[44] The enemy from this viewpoint is the discursive – language which takes time to unfold, and which is therefore prey to verbosity and abstraction, at risk of obfuscating reality rather than revealing it. The discursive, which seems a throwback to the ponderous rationality and well-upholstered prose of the Victorian age, is the verbal equivalent of the idea of historical progress, and both must be repelled. Narrative is disrupted even at the level of the sentence, as with the late James's bafflingly convoluted syntax.

Language is bound fast to temporal process; but there may be ways of deploying it which try to outflank this fate, so that the poem becomes an object we can take in all at once, like a piece of sculpture. We have seen already that space for some modernists begins to take over from time. The paradigm of poetry is no longer music, an art form which from a modernist

MODERNISM

standpoint has the advantage of saying absolutely nothing but the drawback of taking some time to do so. Music tells a kind of story, even if it is without content. We have seen already, however, that modernism does not generally share realism's trust in narrative, any more than it harbours a faith in the upward trek of history. Instead, it is inclined to the cyclical, eternal or instantaneous. 'An "Image"', remarks Ezra Pound, 'is that which presents an intellectual and emotional complex in an instant of time.'[45] It is real, he adds, because we can know it directly, whereas discourse interposes its ungainly bulk between the reader and reality. Communication is instant, visceral and intuitive, rather than clogged by a freight of definitive meanings. Reading a poem is more like being punched in the nose than drawn into a dialogue.

If there is the laconic, however, there is also the loquacious. You can pile language on with deliberate profuseness, in the manner of Gerard Manley Hopkins, J.M. Synge or William Faulkner, in the hope that some of it at least will stick. You can cram your text with too much sense rather than with too little, which is one source of modernist obscurity. If words are perfidious, laying your meaning on with a trowel might do just as well as the chaste clarity of the Imagists. Both styles of writing react against the nerveless prose of everyday life, albeit in opposite directions. Alternatively, like the Symbolists, you can try to cut language loose from reality, severing the bond between the sign and the thing. The word can then become the medium of some higher spiritual reality, transcending its

WORDS AND THINGS

everyday functions in order to put us in touch with the infinite. Dadaist nonsense poetry, the production of pure sound and the Surrealists' so-called automatic writing are different versions of this project, as signifiers are prised loose from their meanings or signifieds.

The Dadaists came up with so-called bruitism, in which everyday objects were used as musical instruments. In one such Dadaist spectacular, typewriters, kettle drums, motor horns, bells, babies' rattles and saucepan lids were used to evoke the awakening of a city. This is still a form of representation; but once the sign or sound is free of the task of reproducing reality, it can become a thing in its own right. It can become, in a word, what music had been all along. Relieved of the burden of denoting objects or states of affairs, language can now meditate on its own material substance – on its sound, shape, tone, rhythm and texture – in what the Russian Formalists call an act of 'estrangement' or 'defamiliarisation'.[46] There is a similar tendency in the visual arts, not least in the Cubist collage. Collage revolutionises the range of materials on which art may draw: paper, cloth, zinc, wood, tinfoil, oilcloth, canvas, playing cards, postage stamps, candlesticks, newspapers and the like. But it also draws attention to the texture and density of these stray odds and ends, estranging everyday objects and plucking artistic value out of the rubble of the commonplace. It was a technique which was to influence the Russian Constructivists, whose particular brand of anti-art we shall be considering later.

MODERNISM

The literary for the Formalists is language freshly conscious of itself, words which flaunt their own material properties; and the effect of this, as we have seen, is to refresh our sense of the everyday world, which has become blunted and 'automatised'. By making the sign strange, the reality it denotes becomes more palpable and perceptible. In deviating from linguistic norms which have grown stale, literature lets us feel the world on our pulses again. In the words of one leading Formalist theorist, Viktor Shklovsky, who speaks of 'the resurrection of the word',[47] it makes the stone stonier. Gertrude Stein remarked of her much-quoted line 'a rose is a rose is a rose' that it made the rose red for the first time in English poetry for a hundred years.[48] Estranging the familiar would seem a purely negative kind of aesthetics, yet it is a moral and political project as well as a poetic one. Literature, it would appear, is the solution to alienation. The modern social order has grown abstract, its politics and bureaucracy cut adrift from everyday sensory existence; and the point of literature is to alienate the alienation – to 'make strange', and thus freshly tangible, a world in which experience itself has become as routinised as an industrial production belt.

There is, however, a much-noted ambiguity in Formalist poetics. It is not always clear whether what is being 'defamiliarised' is the sign itself or its referent. Is it the word 'stone', the concept of it or the actual stone on the beach which is bursting with fresh vitality? Or does the first form of estrangement give rise to the latter two? The equivocation is important, since it

102

WORDS AND THINGS

points to different ways in which language can de-contaminate itself. On the one hand, as we have just seen, it can abandon the irksome task of depicting reality and become loftily autonomous of it. Or it can reflect how things are, but in ironic, self-conscious style, pointing to the gap between the sign and the thing, or the work and the world. In doing so, it can alert us to the limits of its own representational powers. It would seem that any valid reproduction must somehow reckon into itself the ultimate impossibility of what it tries to do. The poem or novel becomes a kind of meta-language which comments on the confines of its own discourse.

There is, however, a quite different possibility. If much modernist art is more abstract than the work of its realist forebears, some of it is also more densely material. If you are troubled by the gap between signs and things, you can ram your language up against reality until the two are seamlessly united. One can trace this strategy all the way from the Soviet Constructivists to twentieth-century 'concrete' poetry, from William Carlos Williams's 'No ideas but in the things' to the poetry of Seamus Heaney. Williams's celebrated slogan is prefigured by a statement in the Soviet journal *Art of the Commune* in 1918: 'Not ideas but a real object is the aim of all true creativity.'[49]

A similar policy can be found in the fondness of Ezra Pound and his fellow Imagists for the Chinese or Japanese ideogram, which they see as a fusion of sign and thing, meaning and object. One of the most influential critical movements

MODERNISM

of modern times, that of the Cambridge critic F.R. Leavis and his pioneering journal *Scrutiny*, holds that language is at its most authentic when it somehow 'enacts' or incarnates the things it speaks of. The English language in Leavis's view is blessed with the singular good fortune of being more capable of this achievement than such ill-starred languages as French.[50] One can also lend language a certain thickness by immersing it in the gross and squalid, as with naturalistic novelists such as Émile Zola. The Chilean poet Pablo Neruda calls for a form of poetry which would be 'ravaged by the labour of our hands as by an acid, saturated with sweat and smoke, a poetry that smells of urine and white lilies, a poetry on which every human activity, permitted or forbidden, has imprinted its mark'.[51] Another commentator praises the Russian Futurist poets for deploying 'words and combinations of words which literally reek of everyday life. There are those which smell of it and those which have a faint odour of it, but the smell of everyday life is in almost every word we use.'[52] No doubt 'literally' here is not to be taken literally.

Either, then, one can turn from daily life to the self-contained sign, finding one's salvation in art or language; or one can move into a deeper intimacy with everyday existence, allowing it to saturate one's speech. On the one hand, art may become abstract and formalistic, in revolt against the messy contingencies of a shapeless world. In the work of a painter like Wassily Kandinsky, pure abstract form, which now becomes the very content of the artwork, issues a spiritual rebuke

WORDS AND THINGS

to an age of materialism. Abstraction is thus itself a form of politics, of however negative a kind. The less realist content a canvas displays, the more critical it becomes of the world it repels. Yet we have seen already that the commodity, too, is a kind of abstraction, so that abstract art colludes with the sphere of capitalist production in the act of fending it off. It mirrors a world in which the abstract has become an objective reality. And if mirroring the world as it actually exists is the task of realism, then abstraction in art becomes the new form of realism.

On the other hand, art may strike against the rationalised nature of the late bourgeois world by taking a turn to the concrete: to vivid immediacies, blood and earth, the visceral regions, primitive cults, the life of the peasantry, the exotic South Sea Island, the fleeting impression or its own material substance. Modernism is an art of the immediate, which is hard to convey in words, as well as a baffled effort to give voice to the infinite, which is even harder. In fact, for some Romantic thinkers the two forms of cognition go hand in hand. The knowledge we reap from stroking a rose petal defeats all abstract concepts, and so is the best intimation we have of the transcendent. If the former cuts beneath everyday rationality, the latter rises above it. As for the literary sign, it is material either because it exists as a thing in itself, or because it is a sensitive medium of the sensory world. The distinction is relevant to the question of gender. The sign or poem as pure, integral and autonomous is really a version of the phallus, in

MODERNISM

the Lacanian sense of an illusory wholeness or impossible fantasy of self-completeness. The sign as the word made flesh is a more feminine mode – though one should note that there can also be something stereotypically masculine about the cult of the concrete.[53]

The two cases would seem mutually incompatible, but the contrast between them is deceptive. This is because there is no such thing as a language which embodies actual objects. All language is abstract, including 'The Rottweiler has just torn a chunk out of my thigh', which is no closer to reality than any of the other sentences in this book. The relation between words and things is not a spatial one. Take these superb lines from John Keats's 'To Autumn':

> To bend with apples the moss'd cottage-trees,
> And fill all fruit with ripeness to the core;
> To swell the gourd, and plump the hazel shells
> With a sweet kernel; to set budding more,
> And still more, later flowers for the bees,
> Until they think warm days will never cease,
> For summer has o'er-brimmed their clammy cells.

Given this lusciously sensuous language, it is easy to believe that we can actually feel these natural processes as they occur. But this is a trompe l'oeil. What we experience is the materiality of the language itself – the physical effort of pronouncing these densely textured lines with their closely packed assonances and

WORDS AND THINGS

alliterative effects, which then puts us in mind of material reality itself. The relationship is one of analogy, not reflection. So the autonomous sign turns out to be referential after all. Simply by focusing on its own material nature, language succeeds in evoking the feel of the world around us.

Yet it is not only language which becomes autonomous. For certain currents of modernist thought, this is true of art itself. Kant's *Critique of Pure Reason* (1781) demonstrates how reason patrols its own borders and marks out its own limits, distinguishing what is appropriate to it from what is improper; and the same is true of art, which must attend to what is pure and peculiar about itself rather than to what is simply external. In this sense, art, like reason, must be conscious of its own constraints. It must include, so to speak, a critical theory of itself, which in some modernist works, as we have seen, takes the form of an ironic awareness of their own artifice. The distinction between art and life is drawn within the work itself. One should note, too, that the autonomy of the work is closely bound up with its unity. Because all of its features are tightly integrated, each locked into place by the concerted pressure of the others, it as though they face inwards towards each other rather than outwards to the world. In turning its back on that reality, the work issues a mute protest against it. Yet at the same time it models a form of subjectivity which belongs to the very bourgeois world it repudiates: the idea of the self as solitary and self-determining, beholden to no law but its own.

MODERNISM

It is important to be clear that the autonomy of art refers not in the first place to a mistaken way of viewing artefacts, detaching them from their historical contexts. There are indeed such tendencies in modernist theory, but the autonomy of art is an historical fact before it is a form of misperception. In any case, placing things in their historical context is by no means always a radical procedure. At least as much historicist thought has sprung from the political right as from the left. For art to be autonomous means that it has been cut loose from any significant social function. In what one might broadly call pre-modern civilisation, art could serve a range of such ends. The artist might be the genealogist of his tribe, a bard with formidable political authority, a monk illuminating manuscripts in the service of the church, an author of masques for the royal court, a propagandist in the pay of the government or a satirist in the pay of the political opposition, a composer, choirmaster or musician employed by the church, a painter of flattering portraits of the landed aristocracy, a decorator of their palaces, designer of their gardens or state-employed architect. One thinks of John Milton: epic poet, political propagandist, religious controversialist, doughty apologist for civil rights and secretary for foreign languages in Oliver Cromwell's government.

As far as the public role of the artist is concerned, consider the difference between W.B. Yeats and the 'decadent' English aesthetes with whom he hung out in Soho bars as a young man. For this group, literary art had largely ceased to be a

WORDS AND THINGS

public affair. Alfred Tennyson, whose poem *In Memoriam* (1850) was Queen Victoria's favourite bedside reading, was probably the last major public poet in England, rather as Dickens was a universally acclaimed popular entertainer despite his fiction being at the same time an example of 'high' art. As an Irish author, however, Yeats was caught up in very different history. Writing at a time of political revolution and civil war in his country, embroiled for a while in the nationalist cause, director of the Irish national theatre and inheritor of a legacy of the poet as public rhetorician, Yeats was able to adopt the role of cultural commissar as well as poet and playwright, becoming an activist in the cultural politics of his time and later a senator in the Irish Free State.

Something of this context is conveyed in the traditional nature of his poetic forms, which can read as though his poetry were to be declaimed rather than privately consumed. These are works animated by a sense of an audience, however occasionally idealised. The integrity of their syntax, in contrast with the fragmented verse of an Eliot, speaks of a specific historical location and sense of audience.[54] Yeats can still speak of 'we Irish', addressing an imaginary community and drawing on what he regards, however dubiously, as a body of myths and symbols which he and his readership have in common. His poem 'The Fisherman' (1916) acknowledges that the contemporary public is something of a rough beast, but also dreams of a future in which he will write for a more responsive readership. If his work is not yet wholly readable, it may

MODERNISM

become so in changed historical circumstances. Like some other Romantic poets, Yeats must help to create the conditions in which his work can be fruitfully received, which includes the task of political transformation.

It is with the growing importance of the commercial market that the traditional social uses of literary art are gradually eclipsed. Once they become thoroughly locked into general commodity production, most artworks are released from their traditional functions within church, court, state and nobility into the anonymous freedom of the marketplace. One disquieting consequence of this is that the buyers of your literary wares are rendered arbitrary and anonymous, a fact which can show up in the style and form of your work. You can no longer be sure who you are addressing. Your writing is no longer declaimed by a bard, passed in manuscript form around a courtly circle or read by the members of your club or coffeehouse. Instead, it is consumed by anyone with the money to buy it and the taste to appreciate it. Ironically, then, the autonomy of art is largely a result of its integration into the capitalist mode of production. In a further irony, art has no sooner been absorbed into commodity production than it launches an eloquent polemic against the social order of which it is part. From the radical Romantics to a whole span of nineteenth-century European novelists, it poses some unsettling questions to the civilisation from which it springs. The fact that it is no longer an instrument of social, political or ecclesiastical authority lends it a licence to protest against the philistine conditions which encircle it.

WORDS AND THINGS

The modern category of the aesthetic, which emerges roughly at the time when the work of art is becoming merchandise in the marketplace, suggests that art is now a specialist area of inquiry, and as such reflects the work's new-found autonomy. Artworks have laws of their own, which it is the task of aesthetics to examine. Artistic production and consumption also evolve their own specialised institutions – the salon, library, studio, museum, gallery, house of culture and the like – which allow them to constitute a sphere in their own right, and so to embed themselves in the public life of modern societies while maintaining a protective distance from it. Yet this enclave is also one in which values that run counter to the logic of the marketplace – the sensuous, erotic, creative, imaginative, non-instrumental – can be cultivated; so that for the first time in its career, at least on any sizeable scale, art becomes a form of social critique. It is one of the places where values expelled from market society can take up a precarious home; and from that vantage point it can speak out against a social order which has precious little use for it other than as a potentially lucrative investment.

In one sense, autonomy represents a genuine emancipation. Art is no longer a compliant servant of the sovereign powers. Instead, it is free to explore a rich diversity of forms and subjects, though the price it pays for this emancipation is steep. It achieves its freedom only at the cost of becoming socially dysfunctional, pushed to the margins of a newly emergent industrial capitalist order. It becomes, so to speak, privatised, a fate

MODERNISM

which has already befallen religion with the rise of Protestant-ism, and which as the modern age unfolds will be increasingly true of sexuality. The artist is becoming an outsider, a bohemian or an internal exile, a destiny which would have been unthink-able for Virgil or Milton, Goethe or Pope. Stereotypically, he is no longer a public figure but a marginal, sometimes reclusive character – vaguely dissident, disdainful of conventional mo-res, spiritually aloof and often enough without a penny to his name. He may be marked by his monkish dedication to the sacred business of art, sacrificing worldly success and domestic fulfilment to the solitary task of sculpting an image or search-ing for hours for the mot juste. Art is now a personal vocation, not a pastime or public ceremony.

In the absence of a familiar readership which shares its way of seeing, the work of art grows introverted and obscure. Its obscurity is deepened by its dealing in the cryptic and ambig-uous, inevitable aspects of a world in which there is no stable foundation or commonly accepted frame of reference. You can, however, turn the difficulty of your art to fruitful use. Thrust to the edges of social existence, the modernist artist exacts his revenge by depriving his fellow citizens of the kitschy or formulaic works with which many of them feel most at home. Instead, he forces them to labour for their enjoyment.

If the artwork is linked to its readers not so much by estab-lished social relations as by the chanciness of commercial ones, it may be tempted to turn its back on its faceless audience and delve instead into its own solitary depths. 'Sometimes you

WORDS AND THINGS

would think I was writing for the public,' smirks Beckett's character Molloy. Henry James speaks scathingly in his short story 'Greville Fane' (1892) of 'the public we [are] condemned to address'. In any case, for an artwork to be accessible to its readers is for it to be open-ended, in which case it must abandon the attempt to be a self-enclosed object. Readers will come up with interpretations of a poem or novel that are beyond the work's own power to determine. To take itself as its own audience – to comment obliquely on its own techniques, growing self-involved and introspective – might then be the only solution to hand. A striking amount of modernist writing is about art and artists. If other subjects seem too run of the mill, one can always write about the triumphs and tribulations of the creative process itself, or make your narrative an allegory of such matters.

Since artistic production now has little function beyond the twin imperatives of private expression and commercial profit, the work feels ungrounded and gratuitous. In this it resembles human beings, to whose existence there is also no necessity. This is certainly one source of modernist angst. As we have seen, the authentic artwork is then one which conveys something of its own contingent nature, and to do so ranks among its various forms of irony. There is no narrative that must at all costs be recounted, as there is for history's sacred scriptures. Any old story will do. Samuel Beckett may launch a tale, abort it abruptly for an unrelated anecdote and then casually jettison that in turn, to show that he is simply cobbling together these

MODERNISM

fragments of fiction as he goes along. His narrators would seem too spiritually drained and depleted to sustain a coherent storyline. The conventional assumption that art is a form of communication is called into question, not least when the paradigm of such communication has become the newspaper or the advertisement. Yet if the human subject is increasingly in pieces, it is also hard to see art as a form of self-expression. Who or what is being expressed?

To see the work of art as an isolated object may seem a peculiarly sterile form of perception. Yet for the late nineteenth-century Symbolists, it is just this autonomy which lends art a universal dimension. If the work is entirely self-contained, then it would seem to be a microcosm of the universe itself, which similarly lacks an exterior. You can therefore find in a thing's self-identity – in the mind-warping fact that a paperweight or a tiger cub is purely, unequivocally itself – a glimpse of the self-identity of the cosmos itself. This is why William Blake can see eternity in a grain of sand, or Gerard Manley Hopkins can find a trace of divinity in the so-called inscape or essence of things. When Ursula Brangwen peers down a microscope at a tiny cell in D.H. Lawrence's novel *The Rainbow*, she sees it as a 'gleaming triumph of infinity'. Pure singularity is a profound mystery. Yet on this view it is also the surest access we can have to the absolute.

If the artwork's curving back upon itself smacks of narcissism, it may also signify a form of utopia. Because the artefact does not need to exist, it is released from the shackles of necessity in a way

WORDS AND THINGS

that nature and civilisation are not. In its artifice lies its salvation. It can offer itself as sheer gift and gratuity, a minor miracle which springs from nowhere and strives towards no particular destination, a momentary rupture of the laws of a drearily deterministic universe. 'When man acts he is a puppet,' claims Oscar Wilde in 'The Critic as Artist' (1891). 'When he describes he is a poet.'[55] To be free is to create, and to create is to be a criminal or immoralist, flouting the dictates of the social and natural worlds. This is one reason why so many avant-garde artists are in love with the random and fortuitous. It is a refutation of the idea of destiny. And since destiny is usually disagreeable, one might consider it well worth resisting. Yet if the act of creation is miraculous, a godlike conjuring of something out of nothing, it cannot be represented, so that art is bound to remain blind to its moment of origin.

The aesthetic artefact also hints at utopia in its sheer uselessness. The useful is the ugly, protests Théophile Gautier. Art is the enemy of utility.[56] If it has been stripped of its time-honoured social functions, it can turn this deprivation to advantage, pluck a virtue from necessity, by maintaining that pointlessness is its very point. It exists purely for its own delight, and thus anticipates a future in which people might be able to do the same. Simply by existing, art represents a critique of instrumental reason. It holds out the promise that there remains something whose raison d'être is not to be bought and sold, even if being marketed turns out to be its own miserable fate. Besides, by ceasing to have

MODERNISM

extraneous uses – to glorify God, celebrate the tribe's military victories and so on – it is set free to investigate its own forms and materials, finding fresh potentials in the stuff from which it is fashioned.

In this respect, modernism is the moment when literature comes to be about words, painting about paint and sculpture about stone. This apparently sterile self-centredness, however, is also an opportunity for experiment and innovation, as art breaks through the confines of social duty or moral exhortation to attend solely to the task of being itself. Victorian writing, for example, is constrained by the fact that it is expected to be morally edifying. When a large sector of the population is potentially disaffected, it is imprudent to spread gloom and despondency. Pessimism is politically dangerous. Hence the stereotypical happy ending of the Victorian novel, which is not allowed to infect Jane Eyre with typhoid in the final paragraph or show Fagin bribing his way off death row. It is a convention which is abandoned only with the fiction of Thomas Hardy. From then on, novels will tend to conclude on a much less affirmative note, or not really conclude at all. The last words of Lawrence's *Women in Love* are ' "I don't believe that," he answered.'

The finest of all theorists of modernism, the German philosopher Theodor Adorno, is a fervent apologist for the autonomous work of art, but has no doubt of the exorbitant cost that it exacts.[57] By distancing itself from the rest of social reality, the autonomous work, as we have seen, is able to act as a

WORDS AND THINGS

form of critique, in the way that a more socially integrated art – a courtly sonnet or Constructivist rocking chair – finds it less easy to do. Yet if the artwork's distance from other social institutions allows room for such a critique, it also threatens to undercut its force. There are other contradictions to be considered as well. If the work of art is realist in content, it risks being complicit with a corrupt reality; for it to retreat into pure form, however, is a privilege that political leftists like Adorno can only grudgingly endorse. There is, to be sure, a utopian element to such purity, one which can issue a powerful rebuff to prevailing social values. In doing so, however, art becomes in its own way as much a reified object as the commodities against which it protests. In drawing its various elements together in a way which respects their integrity, it represents a challenge to dominative reason; yet in doing so it cannot avoid reminding us of that reason's remorseless drive for totality. Art, in a word, is impaled on the horns of a set of impossible dilemmas, aware that to reject utopia is just as unpalatable as to aspire to it, that negating the actual is as essential as it is ineffectual, and that embracing the bourgeois world is every bit as untenable as turning one's back on it.

A valid art, Adorno insists, yields us a 'negative knowledge of reality'. 'A successful work', he writes, 'is not one which resolves objective contradictions in a spurious harmony, but which expresses the idea of harmony negatively by embodying the contradictions, pure and uncompromised, in its innermost structure.'[58] 'It is not the office of art to spotlight

MODERNISM

alternatives,' he argues against the politically engaged writing of Bertolt Brecht and Jean-Paul Sartre, 'but to resist by its form alone the course of the world, which permanently puts a pistol to men's heads.'[59] Adorno's writing on modernism represents aesthetics at the end of its tether, with something of the agonised extremity of the works it investigates. It is less a theory of art than of its near impossibility in late capitalist conditions.

If the modernist artwork is reluctant to be taken for a commodity, it is equally wary of being treated as a natural object. In a world in which truth has splintered into a myriad of conflicting standpoints, art seeks to 'denaturalise' itself – to make us aware that it represents one version of reality among many. Unlike certain classical realist works, it has no unimpeachable claim to authority. One thinks of the multifaceted objects of Cubism, viewed from several clashing perspectives simultaneously. There is also irony, montage, collage, the use of multiple narrative standpoints and other such interactional techniques. By 'baring the device', in Formalist jargon – confessing through its ironic self-consciousness that it is no more than a contrivance – art refuses the allure of absolute truth in a world in which all truth appears contingent and provisional. In an era of fascist and Stalinist dogma, agnosticism begins to look appealing. Samuel Beckett, who fought against fascism in the ranks of the French Resistance, remarked that his favourite word was 'perhaps'.[60] Like his guerrilla activities, it was intended as a riposte to the absolutist and authoritarian.

WORDS AND THINGS

This is not, as it happens, an agnosticism one should endorse too readily, however congenially it may ring in liberal or postmodern ears. For one thing, one should not make a bugbear of the term 'absolute'. It is absolutely true that most people with very small feet tend to have less general knowledge than most people with large ones,[61] but the word 'absolutely' does not pull much weight in this context. To claim that something is absolutely wrong is to claim that it is wrong independent of any context one might think up in order to justify it. There is no situation one can dream up to justify the rape of small children or the unleashing of nuclear weapons on a civilian population, as there are contexts in which one could justify lying, assassination or stealing from supermarkets.

What is on the wane with modernism is the classical realist faith that there is an order inherent in reality. This is one reason why the Surrealists were fascinated with bizarre juxtapositions of objects, or with throwing art open to what they oxymoronically called the 'laws of chance'. One thinks also of T.S. Eliot's view of the Metaphysical poets as yoking the most heterogeneous ideas violently together. As long as there is assumed to be a coherent structure immanent in the world, the work of art has only to mirror this design in order to achieve some unity in itself. It is this which we know as classical realism. If this is no longer the case, however, there are two possibilities. Either art gives up on the idea of unity altogether, which is as true of some avant-garde artists as it is of a great many postmodernist ones; or it arbitrarily imposes a pattern

MODERNISM

on a reality which it knows to be formless in itself. In order not to stand convicted of bad faith, however, the artwork must somehow show its hand in this respect, confessing that the cohesion of its subject matter is no more than a construct. It must point to the gap between the disorder of the world and its own shapely form. Joyce's title *Ulysses* is one such gesture. A random day in Dublin takes on a highly determinate shape, as contingency is secretly imbued with necessity. But this is only because what happens in the novel is modelled on a Homeric myth; and part of the joke is that this, too, is gratuitous. As an organising principle, another myth might have served just as well.

Modernist works divide roughly between those which subordinate experience to a purity of form, and those which chafe against form in the name of the direct representation of experience. The poetry of Mallarmé is an instance of the former, while Dorothy Richardson's *Pilgrimage* is exemplary of the latter. Phenomenology, which has its roots in the modernist era, seeks to resolve this antithesis by focusing on lived experience but finding within it certain unchanging forms or essences.

Might it still be possible, however, to transform chaos into a new form of order in the everyday world, as well as in art? Can modern art change the world rather than simply negating it? It is to these essentially political questions that we can now turn.

3

THE DEATH OF ART

On the third anniversary of the Bolshevik Revolution, the Russian theatre director Vsevolod Meyerhold restaged the storming of the Winter Palace, using a cast of around 15,000, motor cavalcades, siege guns and a battleship. He had previously taken over whole towns to stage his productions, enlisting the entire population as actors. His plans to celebrate the revolution a year later, with 2,300 infantry, 200 cavalry, motorbikes, aeroplanes and complete tank and artillery regiments along with orchestras and mass choirs, proved beyond even his talent for mass organisation.

There were also those astonishing moments in post-revolutionary Russia when at the Moscow State Theatre one might find Meyerhold, who was later to die in a Stalinist prison camp, at work on a play with music by Shostakovich, script by the Russian Formalist Viktor Shklovsky or the Futurist poet Vladimir Mayakovsky, film effects by Sergei Eisenstein

MODERNISM

and stage designs by the Constructivist artist Vladimir Tatlin. Constructivists such as Aleksandr Rodchenko, El Lissitsky and their colleagues abandoned their studios and went out into the factories in order to harness art to social need. Easel painting was to be put aside for the design of textiles, clothing and furniture. Artists were to manufacture useful objects, not decorative ones. Art and industry would form a seamless whole. If this kind of activity is to be included under the heading of modernism, then the intellectually indolent assumption that all modernist art is 'elitist' stands in urgent need of revision.

Agitprop theatre groups, composed largely of amateur actors and performing without costumes or scenery, took their productions into the countryside to keep the peasantry abreast of new social and political developments in the cities. By 1928, more or less every city in Germany had one or more such troupes, and in the following decade the movement spread to Britain, where one of the best-known groups was based in the city of Salford. Workers' theatre and worker-writers associations, including the English Workers' Theatre Movement, sprang up throughout Europe. In the Soviet Union, poets like Mayakovsky proclaimed their work through megaphones in factory yards, while Cubists and Suprematists decorated Moscow streets and raised revolutionary monuments.

Similarly ambitious projects were to be found in the German Weimar Republic. At the Social Democratic Party theatre in the Berlin of the 1920s, one might find the Marxist

THE DEATH OF ART

and former Dadaist and Expressionist Erwin Piscator directing a drama in which Brecht had a hand, with music by Hanns Eisler or Kurt Weill, film effects by the former Dadaist George Grosz and stage design by the eminent artist and photographer László Moholy-Nagy or the Surrealist Otto Dix. Intent on revolutionising stage design, Piscator introduced ramps, treadmills, placards, catwalks, scaffolding, three-tiered stages, interlocking steps and platforms, cycloramas on vertical rollers, film projectors, loudspeakers and direct addresses to the audience. There were slides and flies, floats and revolves, traps, bridges, lifts and alternative stages. The director's exorbitant love of machinery was typical of the heady left-rationalism of his time, though the treadmills sometimes creaked so loudly that the actors could hardly be heard above them. It was a materialist theatre in more senses than one.

It was also theatre as laboratory as well as entertainment.[1] One could react to what seemed a clapped-out modern rationality either with the irrational, like many a modernist artist, or with the super-rational – with reason in the shape of the latest technology and scientific discoveries. Yet if Piscator's theatre was an arena of investigation, it was also intended to stimulate and enthuse, and so was not without its more sensory attractions. One play, *The Red Review*, mixed music, song, slide-projection, action-painting, acrobatics, sport, rhetoric, film, dance and acting. In another, more macabre production about the First World War, intended to provoke fury and disgust rather than enjoyment, a legless beggar and half a dozen

123

MODERNISM

genuinely disabled men paraded across the stage smeared in blood and dirt, with their missing limbs hanging out of their backpacks.

The talk in cultural circles was of the city and the machine, warfare and the masses, the end of high art and the reconstruction of the human psyche in collective revolutionary terms. A play of the period by J.R. Becher entitled *Workers, Peasants, Soldiers* concludes with the stage direction: 'Weapons are distributed on the stage and further weapons are handed down from the stage among the onlookers.'[2] The actors, having roused and armed the audience, were then supposed to lead them to the local police headquarters and take it by storm. In another of Piscator's productions, the public participated through shouts and speeches, and at the end of the show voted by a show of hands for the repeal of a certain section of the criminal code. It was all a far cry from Noël Coward.

Realist art, by contrast, tends not to acknowledge the reader's or viewer's presence. Things happen as though we were not there. They are self-contained rather than reliant on our response. One reason why we do not suspect Norman Bates of being the murderer in Alfred Hitchcock's film *Psycho* is because he seems genuinely distraught when he discovers the victim's body in the shower. Since there is no other character on the scene to be deceived by his distress, and since we, the audience, are not supposed to be there in any case, we naturally assume that his horror is genuine (which, indeed, it is, though not because he is innocent of the crime).

THE DEATH OF ART

In the Soviet Union in the early 1920s, there were concerts of factory hooters conducted by workers standing on rooftops. A new human sensorium was thought to be evolving, one shaped by the shocks, speed, ephemera and swift combination of sensations of the city, and it was the task of art to lend it expression. This new form of art was epitomised by film, with its quick cuts, multiple viewpoints, montage effects, mass appeal and mechanical basis. Perhaps it was cinema which would bring the outlandish art of the avant-garde home to the people. Brechtian theatre, which at its height was both popular and experimental, avant-garde and working-class, achieved much the same end.

Meyerhold's extravagant productions serve almost as a parody of the practices of the revolutionary avant-gardes, from Futurism and Constructivism to Dada, Surrealism and Situationism. Their aim was not so much to produce a new species of art as to challenge the very category of art itself, a question which high modernism tends not to raise. Is the aesthetic really a category of its own, or should one rather seek to break down the barriers between art and the rest of social existence? This, generally speaking, is a key characteristic of the various avant-gardes which sprang up in the early decades of the twentieth century. One way to demolish the distinction between art and life is to exploit the resources of modern technology in order to strip art of its enchantment, as with the theatre of Piscator and Brecht or the products of Cubism and Constructivism. The magical must give way to the materialist.

125

MODERNISM

We have seen that the era of modernity, at least from the work of Kant onwards, tends to value distinction and division. There are troublesome consequences in store if you confuse theoretical with moral knowledge, or the ethical with the aesthetic. No viewpoint could be further from the post-modernist sensibility, with its championing of the hybrid and eclectic, its consumerist assumption that boundaries and discriminations are deplorable forms of hierarchy or exclusion. It is with the early twentieth-century avant-gardes, however, that the frontiers between the aesthetic, scientific, ethical and political first begin to blur. Art must be hooked up once more with social practice, and the forces which have rendered it dysfunctional overthrown. In the process, art as a distinct phenomenon will wither away.[3]

Whether these projects are to be treated as a branch of modernism in general, or as a distinct development, is a controversial issue. In *The Five Paradoxes of Modernity*, Antoine Compagnon insists on a strict demarcation between the two currents, reviling the various avant-gardes (perhaps in repentance for his own utopian dreams as a student in the Paris of 1968), and treating Baudelaire rather in the manner of a minor deity.[4] In his *The Theory of the Avant-Garde*, by contrast, Renato Poggioli treats modernism and the avant-garde as more or less interchangeable,[5] while in a study of almost the same title Peter Bürger contrasts modernism in general with what he regards as the single most definitive aspect of avant-gardism – its rejection of the whole concept of an

126

THE DEATH OF ART

art institution distinct from other forms of social activity. It is the social location of art, not just its content, which is at stake.

Modernism, Bürger argues, marks the point at which the content of the work of art becomes at one with its institutional status. He means by this that rather as the institution of art leads a life of its own in the modern world, so now do the artworks it produces. They, too, would seem bereft of any very obvious social function. In this sense, modernism resolves a contradiction which can be detected in realism. The realist work is bound to its social context by its content; but it is divorced from that context at an institutional level, since art is now a practice which is largely independent of politics, religion and social affairs. In shedding such social content, then, the modernist artwork can be seen as coming to terms with this discrepancy. The avant-garde, by contrast, represents not simply another form of art, but a critique of art itself. In Bürger's words, it represents 'the self-criticism of art in bourgeois society'.[6]

We have seen already that with the growth of the commercial market, the artwork tends to abandon most of its traditional social functions, not least what one might call its cultic or ritual ones. Its entry into the marketplace strips it of the aura and ceremony with which it was sometimes invested in courtly, aristocratic and ecclesiastical circles – an aura which the modernist artefact seeks to restore in its own more secular way. Art for modernism is once more granted revered status,

MODERNISM

though this time in social and aesthetic terms rather than religious ones. It becomes something of a cult once again, though without the divine significance it once possessed. The artist, as we have seen, becomes a secular priest, but lacks the authority of the traditional cleric. It is this halo of mystery and privilege which the revolutionary avant-gardes are out to demolish with their veneration of the machine.

Part of that halo of mystery stems from the supposedly organic nature of the modernist work – from the complex interdependence of its various parts, which seems to lend it a unique life of its own. The poem, painting or piece of sculpture appears to turn in on itself, as each of its features draws meaning not from any external reality but from the artistic whole. A good deal of avant-garde art, by contrast, is deliberately non-organic, granting its various aspects a high degree of autonomy and allowing them to clash and contrast. Brecht's so-called epic theatre, in which scenes are loosely, contingently interrelated in a form of dramatic montage, is a case in point. Alternatively, an artwork may pluck its components from different contexts and stitch them incongruously together, as in the practice of collage.

By refusing the organic, the avant-garde work also refuses to present itself as natural, and so as inevitable. Instead, it puts its process of production candidly on show, making clear that it is a construct. Instead of unity, it offers us dissonance, fragmentation and contradiction. There are conflicts in the art of, say, Rilke or Borges, but generally speaking the work strives to

THE DEATH OF ART

contain them within a coherent form. For the more militant of the avant-gardists, however, such art remains the prisoner of a classical dream of integrity. Discord must infiltrate the form of the artwork as well as its content, as it does in the case of *Ulysses* or *The Waste Land*. Only thus will the poem or novel be genuinely heterogeneous, which is also true of the post-modern art which emerges in its wake. In rejecting the idea of unity as a form of fetishism, the avant-garde throws out an aesthetic doctrine which has proved remarkably tenacious all the way from Aristotle to I.A. Richards. There are political as well as artistic reasons behind this rejection. Unity suggests that art itself is able to resolve social antagonisms, a task which for revolutionary artists only politics can perform.

'Modernism', writes T.J. Clark, 'is caught interminably between horror and elation at the forces [of modernity] driving it.'[7] Perhaps it is not too simplistic to see modernism proper as registering the horror (Baudelaire, Eliot, Pound) and the avant-garde as feeling the elation (Futurism, Cubism, Constructivism, the Bauhaus). We shall be returning to this contrast later. The critic Marshall Berman sees this divided condition as a feature of modernity itself, with its fraught co-existence of agitation and excitement, self-enlargement and self-derangement, the expansion of the self but also the destruction of personal bonds and moral boundaries. The locus of these contradictions is above all the modern city – at once dynamic and disorienting, intoxicating in its pleasures yet shot through with angst and instability.[8]

MODERNISM

In a commentary on Berman's work, Perry Anderson eloquently summarises Marx's dialectical vision of capitalist modernity:

> On the one hand, capitalism . . . tears down every ancestral confinement and feudal restriction, social immobility and claustral tradition, in an immense clearing operation of cultural and customary debris across the globe. To that process corresponds a tremendous emancipation of the possibility and sensibility of the individual self, now increasingly released from the fixed social status and rigid role-hierarchy of the pre-capitalist past, with its narrow morality and cramped imaginative range. On the other hand, as Marx emphasised, the very same onrush of capitalist economic development also generates a brutally alienated and atomised society, riven by callous economic exploitation and cold social indifference, destructive of every cultural or political value whose potential it has itself brought into being. Likewise, on the psychological plane, self-development could only mean a profound disorientation and insecurity, frustration and despair, *concomitant with* – indeed inseparable from – the sense of enlargement and exhilaration, the new capacities and feelings, liberated at the same time.[9]

For Marx, then, modernity is both a delight and a disaster – a dialectical judgement alien for the most part to the artists we are

THE DEATH OF ART

considering. If some sections of the avant-garde are too bullish and dewy-eyed in their trust in science, rationalism, progress and technology, some of their high modernist colleagues are too disdainful and despondent. Broadly speaking, modernism is too estranged from everyday life, while the avant-garde is too eager to integrate with it. Given that the positive and negative aspects of industrial capitalism are so deeply interwoven, it is hard for either camp to tread a judicious path between mindless dynamism and bitter disenchantment – which is to say, between the Panglosses on the one hand and the Jeremiahs on the other.

Some avant-gardists are full of iconoclasm and panache, but sometimes with a strain of callow triumphalism. The rhapsodic language of the Italian writer Filippo Tommaso Marinetti's first Futurist manifesto of 1909 captures the mood exactly:

> We affirm that the beauty of the world has been enriched by a new form of beauty: the beauty of speed. A racing car with a hood which glistens with large stripes resembling a serpent with explosive breath . . . a roaring automobile that rides on grape-shot – that is more beautiful than the 'Victory of Samothrace' . . . We intended to glorify war – the only hygiene in the world – militarism, patriotism, the destructive gesture of emancipation, beautiful ideas worth dying for, and contempt for woman. We intend to destroy museums, libraries, academies of every sort, and to fight against moralism, feminism, and every utilitarian or

MODERNISM

opportunistic cowardice. We shall sing the great masses, shaken with work, pleasure, or rebellion; we shall sing the multicoloured and polyphonic tidal waves of revolution in the modern metropolis.[10]

Unsurprisingly, the revolution which the author of these adolescent ravings would finally champion was a fascist one.[11] Marinetti was fond of a fight: he claimed that he used to sell the same ticket for his Futurist performances to ten people in order to ensure a fracas at the box office. The fact that he was for a time an ardent supporter of Mussolini suggests that social progressivism and technological innovation do not go spontaneously hand in hand. The disparity between the two may help to explain why the Nazi propagandist Josef Goebbels offered a job to the communist theatre director Erwin Piscator. Technological change can be harnessed to a variety of political agendas, some enlightened and some not. Dynamism and dissonance are by no means inherently virtuous. Nor is the future always an improvement on the present. In any case, a good many Futurists were bohemian dissidents rather than political revolutionaries: strident, macho, posturing, abusive, philistine, belligerent and doctrinaire. Some of these fetishists of the future were convinced that all previous art should be destroyed, along with all libraries and museums. Fiction was suspect, while the literature of fact should reign supreme.

There was a constructive dimension, however, as well as a nihilistic one. The Futurists, along with the more sober-minded

THE DEATH OF ART

Constructivists and Bauhaus artists, were engaged in an historic attempt to transform the meaning of art, the role of the artist and the relations between artists and audiences. If avant-gardism includes the glorification of war and a small-boyish bedazzlement with the latest technological toys, it also encompasses Eisenstein and Brecht, Gropius and Le Corbusier, Vertov and Mayakovsky, worker choirs and popular political theatre, cinema, typography and photo-montage, as well as a ferocious assault on a complacent cultural establishment. The study and studio were to be abandoned for the workshop, factory and laboratory. Tatlin designed a worker's suit which tapered inwards towards the legs so that heat could not escape downwards, while two distinguished female Constructivist designers, Lyubov Popova and Varvara Stepanova, went off to work in textile factories. Popova, who died of scarlet fever in 1924, stemmed from a wealthy Moscow family, studied in Europe and became a Suprematist. She also designed sets and costumes for Meyerhold's theatre and collaborated with the Left Front in the Arts. The three fundamental elements of dress design, she declared, were the ideological, the analytical and the technical, which might come as a surprise to Stella McCartney. Even so, she violated strict Constructivist tenets with the subdued elegance of her skirts and blouses.

Broadly speaking, the Futurists were romantic revolutionaries while the Constructivists were rationalist ones. The square, rectangle and triangle took pride of place in Constructivist clothing. Malevich designed some Suprematist cups and

133

MODERNISM

saucers which were easy on the eye but a lot harder to drink from. Eisenstein, who wanted somewhat bizarrely to film Marx's *Capital*, worked as a designer and poster painter for agitprop theatre, while Rodchenko produced placards, designs and posters for Mayakovsky's volumes of poetry. Mayakovsky himself hailed advertising in the new post-market Soviet economy as a form of industrial and commercial agitation. A group of avant-gardists designed an advertisement for babies' dummies or comforters for the State Rubber Trust, declaring that 'there have never been and are no better dummies. You'll want to suck them until old age.'[12] Flushed with revolutionary- romantic fervour, Futurists decorated city streets and designed mass festivals, revolutionary monuments and tombs for fallen fighters. One Soviet architect envisaged a town of glass and asbestos, built on springs and soaring to the sky. A Temple of Intercourse between Nations was another project which never left the drawing board, along with numerous plans for communal housing. Everywhere one looked there were cubes, cones, cylinders, spheres, segments, radiating lines, brash colours and intersecting surfaces. 'The streets are our brushes, the squares our palettes,' declared an exuberant Mayakovsky.[13]

The various arts were to be synthesised, overriding traditional distinctions between poetry and painting, sculpture and architecture. Photography was fashionable because it combined art and technology, while photo-montage was the invention of the Berlin Dadaists. One of the aims of photography was to see familiar objects from defamiliarising viewpoints, thus

THE DEATH OF ART

expanding one's social consciousness. Tatlin was commissioned to design a monument to the revolution (later named 'Monument to the Third International') which would distil the dynamism of the Bolshevik era. According to a contemporary commentator, it was to be:

> a place of the most intense movement; least of all should one stand still or sit down in it, you must be mechanically taken up, down, carried away against your will, in front of you must flash the powerful laconic phrases of the orator-agitator, and . . . the latest news, decrees, decisions, the latest inventions, an explosion of simple and clear thoughts, creativity, only creativity.[14]

There would also be a film projector for beaming messages on to the clouds, along with a garage to house cars and motorcycles for the distribution of propaganda.

The tower was to be literally a place of movement, consisting as it did of three glass rooms placed one upon another, each of them rotating at a different speed. The lowest room, a cube, was intended for legislative assemblies and turned on its axis at the rate of one revolution a year. The next, pyramid-shaped chamber, intended to house various executive bodies, rotated at the rate of one revolution a month, while the upper cylinder, an office for information and propaganda, would move at the speed of one revolution a day. Leon Trotsky thought the whole thing looked like a beer bottle. Like a good many Constructivist projects, this Swiftian fantasy remained mercifully unrealised. In a period of war and social turmoil, hunger and destitution, marked by drastically low levels of technological development and a widespread lack of materials, equipment and professional training, the avant-gardist imagination overshot the limits of social reality in ways which were both admirable and absurd. What was meant to be eminently practical was often enough academicist fantasy.

An Institute of Artistic Culture was set up in Moscow in 1920, upholding the principle of absolute artistic freedom and open to all students regardless of educational background and attainment. Its aim was to prepare 'highly qualified master artists' for industry – a task deemed so vital that it warranted the deferment of active military service. Its preliminary training programme, however, was denounced by a group of militant Constructivists, who complained that 'there is no whiff of any kind of social task. No posters, caricatures, social satire or grotesque depictions of everyday life – only timeless, spaceless, partyless, "pure", "sacred" painting and sculpture, with its landscapes, still lifes and naked models.'[15]

The Left Front in the Arts was established in the Soviet Union in the early 1920s, with its Futurist, Formalist and Constructivist members bent upon 'the explosion of antiquity' and united in their hostility to symbolist, mimetic and academicist art. So-called production art would see off the aesthetes and dilettantes. There was to be no more talk of creation, with its objectionably theological overtones. The making of an art object was to be

THE DEATH OF ART

more or less on a level with churning out a pair of boots. The anarchic, individualist energies of the artist were to be strictly channelled and collectively organised. Under the influence of Cubism, the leading Constructivist Vladimir Tatlin built reliefs out of wood, planks, ropes, bottles and bits of cloth. Anything from a cheap top hat to a pair of soiled gloves could be nailed together, since their most vital common factor was their materiality. Rules of composition were to be replaced by principles of construction and organisation, while aesthetic taste yielded ground to social function. Clarity, simplicity, economy and functionality were the key concepts. So, too, was transparency: objects should no longer conceal the way they were made but (in Formalist idiom) lay bare the device, letting their audience in on the secret of their inner structure. Realism was taboo: the role of art was not to depict the world but to change it. Production, not reproduction, was the watchword. Art was a hammer, not a mirror. Leftist artists were to regard themselves as 'industrialists in art' as well as political agitators.

Worship of money gave way in some quarters to adulation of the machine. In fact, a good deal of modernism can be seen as a shift from the human to the inhuman – from the organic to the inorganic, the sentimental to the analytical, personality to impersonality, purity of form rather than lifelike content. Some of the Futurists and Constructivists, ironically enough for leftists, were enthusiasts of so-called Fordism and Taylorism, the American 'sciences' of mechanising and standardising industrial labour for the more efficient exploitation of those who

MODERNISM

performed it. Standardisation would minimise the role of subjective criteria in the production process. Meyerhold practised a form of theatrical Taylorism known as biomechanics, cutting out superfluous gestures, motions and expressions as though his actors were production-line workers. They were methods derived not only from Taylorist techniques but also from circus acrobatics and Chinese and Japanese theatre. Passion and psychology were to be sacrificed to a scientific form of acting, from which Bertolt Brecht was to learn much of his trade. The emphasis was on skill, not sincerity, action rather than emotion. Feelings could be left to the middle classes, who had the leisure to indulge them.

Some avant-garde artists, as we have seen, were enthused by the idea of dehumanisation. In their view, there could be no high-modernist flight from the world into the depths of the private subject, since the subject itself was now in the process of being measured and mechanised. Subjectivity, so to speak, had been taken into public ownership. Some of the Constructivists regarded humans as machines to be dismantled and efficiently reconstructed. An Institute for the Scientific Organisation of Work and the Mechanisation of Man was established in the early years of the Soviet Union. It was a prolific period for the establishing of institutes with portentous titles which then sank without trace. The epoch of the bourgeois subject, locked in its own unfathomably intricate depths, was now supposedly at a close. What would kill it off, in an ironic twist, was the technology to which bourgeois society itself had

THE DEATH OF ART

given birth. In this post-human world, people were to be seen as functions of social forces, anonymous, collective and interchangeable. To be released from the prison house of subjectivity was a precious emancipation, not a ruinous loss. In challenging bourgeois culture, then, one could find oneself complicit with its own economic base, since nothing affirms the new more than the capitalist mode of production. The artistic demand for novelty, mechanisation and impersonality turns the economic logic of capitalism against the bourgeois civilisation it breeds.

Even those brands of modernism which detested the machine could still be entranced by the impersonal, if of a less technocratic kind than the mechanisation of Man. For authors like Eliot and Lawrence, to plunge into the interior of the self is to encounter a bedrock of being which is collective rather than personal, whether one calls it the European mind, the Jungian archetype, the enduring wisdom of the common people or spontaneous-creative life. You can undercut the callow ego of everyday existence either by deep subjectivity or by an austere impersonality. It is possible to see Expressionism as an intensely subjective experience of the loss of subjectivity. Moreover, if the work of art is to be autonomous, it must be impersonal in the sense of being cut loose from its author as well as from its historical context. Trust the tale, not the teller, as Lawrence counsels. The self has become too volatile and elusive to offer a reliable reference point. Perhaps it is no more than the irregular flow of its experiences, too shifting and

MODERNISM

fragmentary to provide the firm foundation which René Descartes had proposed for it. In modernist circles in general, there is a shift away from the Romantic cult of self-expression, which now seems as passé as the iambic pentameter. Eliot's path-breaking essay 'Tradition and the Individual Talent' regards art as an escape from personality rather than a release of it. It is a smack at the Romantic and liberal humanist pieties on which he had waged war from the outset.

Much modernist writing, to be sure, involves a turn from the object to the subject. There is a shift from reality to experience, from the way things are to the way they feel. Nineteenth-century positivism yields to twentieth-century phenomenology. Reality may be hard to decipher, but one's immediate experience of it is one of the few lingering certainties in an unstable world. Yet even when the subject remains valued, it is no longer the coherent, self-determining, sharply individualised self of high modernity. Instead, art is in search of fresh forms of subjectivity, beyond the threadbare discourse of 'ego', 'character' and 'personality'. If subjectivity is to thrive, the classical self, with its coercive will and carefully policed frontiers, must be abandoned. The subject is now less a unified substance than a field without either a centre or clear boundaries, forever merging into objects or spreading into other subjects, fluid and indeterminate. A writer like Woolf conjures superlative art from this vision, yet one should not fall prey to the fallacy that fluidity is a virtue in itself. One does not want to hear that the decision to repeal your execution by firing

140

THE DEATH OF ART

squad is still in a fluid state. Nor is fluidity the same as freedom, as postmodernism tends to assume. It is the market-place which regards constant flux as the natural condition of humanity.

For a number of modernist artists, then, impersonality is not the opposite of subjectivity but what you discover when you delve to its depths. At the root of the subject itself lie certain great anonymous forces: language, myth, race, archetype, spirit, history, material conditions, genetic inheritance, the Life Force, the unconscious and so on, powers which live us far more than we live them. We are no longer the self-fashioning creatures we once imagined ourselves to be. In D.H. Lawrence's view, the human subject is constituted by that which is not itself – indeed, by that which is profoundly strange to it. It is not true, as an entrenched tradition of Western thought holds, that we are intimate with ourselves but strangers to others. On the contrary, one of Lawrence's most cherished convictions is that we are strangers to ourselves. The self is a law unto itself, rather than unto oneself. It is not something we possess, or whose course we can strenuously determine. We are stewards, not proprietors, of ourselves. The self is a mysterious gift which comes to us from the Infinite, and which we should nurture as tenderly as if it were the being of another. Lawrence was a racist, sexist, homophobic anti-Semite, which is no doubt why he is not much read today. Yet he was also a writer of genius, however fitfully, who was possessed of some absorbing ideas. His sense of the self is echoed by Simone Weil, who

MODERNISM

wrote in the year in which she starved herself to death that 'so far from it being his person, what is sacred in a human being is the impersonal in him. Everything which is impersonal in man is sacred, and nothing else.'[16]

What Lawrence calls spontaneous-creative life resists the violence of the dominative will, and will have its own sweet way whatever our conscious intentions. At the very core of the self lies that which is implacably other to it, and which we deny only at the cost of a certain blasphemy. The roots of identity, for Lawrence as for Freud, lie unfathomably deeper than mere personality, which is why he comes to dismiss the realist conception of character as purely two-dimensional.[17] We need to be vigilantly, vulnerably open to the stirrings of spontaneous life both in ourselves and others. The price of this wise passiveness, however, is that it leaves little room for human agency. Modernism of this kind is a species of anti-humanism. The Romantic vision of art as the self-expression of a subject, one active in the world and intent on transforming it, is obsolete. The language of power, individual genius, self-realisation and a harmoniously developed humanity no longer has the ring of authenticity, as it did in the decades around the French Revolution. The keywords are now irony, scepticism, contingency, ambiguity, impersonality and indeterminacy. The middle class has passed from its revolutionary to its post-revolutionary phase. The idiom of self-realisation is salvaged to some extent by the avant-garde, but now in collectivised form.

142

THE DEATH OF ART

What is gradually on the wane, then, with the diffusing and dislodging of the subject, is a sense of the self as agent, constituted by its activity in the world alongside other such transformative beings. If the avant-garde tends to be hyperactive, some modernist artists find the whole concept of action profoundly problematic. Because social reality appears either inert and impenetrable, or fragile and evanescent, the subject lacks an accessible object with which it can enter into dialogue, confirming its own identity in the process. This is one of several reasons why it begins to implode. Confronted by forces beyond its comprehension, as well as beyond its control, it can no longer lend itself a degree of coherence in the act of shaping the world into significant form.

It was craft, not art, which was fundamental to revolutionary aesthetics – a form of labour which demands a sophisticated knowledge of materials, a faultless eye and hand and a meticulous sense of social function. It also bridged the traditional gap between art and manual work. This, in effect, was the aim of the Russian Constructivists of the 1920s, who in rejecting the aesthetic for the austerely functional declared themselves to be 'fighting for the placard, for the illustration, the advertisement, photo- and cine-montage, i.e. for those types of utilitarian-representational art which could be art for the masses, put into effect by means of machine techniques, and closely tied to the urban industrial workers'.[18] Craft was to be mechanised and collectivised, as the individual artisan at his work bench was swept away by mass production. In both the Soviet

MODERNISM

Union and Weimar Germany, the public arts of architecture and town planning surged to the fore. Artists also threw themselves into campaigns against illiteracy, in a Russia in which 76 per cent of the population in 1914 were unable to read or write. The Futurists demanded that all art schools, galleries and theatres should be independent of the state and come under the control of artists themselves.

Some of the avant-garde sought to press art into the service of political revolution; but many of its members were also intent on revolutionising art itself, and the two aims were not always mutually compatible. The masses were accustomed to realism, not abstract concoctions of wood and wire. Rather than admiring such experiments, the workers, soldiers and peasants of the early Russian soviets were more likely to be enthused by the Italian Futurists' demand for wholesome, everyday subject matter in poetry, turning from 'the primitive and the savage, the sylvan and the rustic . . . the adoration of the gloomy, the mouldy, the filthy and decrepit . . . the exaltation of decay, disease, failure and suicide'.[19] The Russian Futurists, the only group of artists to cooperate wholeheartedly with the new Soviet regime, experimented with the visual and material aspects of literature – with books, paper, illustrations, dust jackets, calligraphy and typography. Some of them were also eager to transform language itself, producing so-called 'transsense' poetry and contriving new effects of rhythm and sound, bending syntax and promoting new forms of punctuation, not much of which would seem instantly accessible on the factory

THE DEATH OF ART

floor. It was what one Futurist called a 'phonetic revolution'. Surely, he asks, 'we communists are looking at the world anew and don't we have the desire to rechristen, give new names to everything that has been despoiled by the odious political past? . . . The striving to rename and form new words is inevitable in a revolutionary age.'[20]

Paradoxically, then, nonsense poetry and mass insurgency went hand in hand, in theory if not in practice. Mayakovsky splintered conventional syntax rather as the Bolsheviks dismantled the tsarist state, exploiting the elliptical, abrasive language of the street rather than the refined discourse of the salon. Grammar was a bridle on verbal inventiveness which must be cast aside. If the word was to be emancipated alongside the workers and peasantry, textbook orthodoxies had to be scrapped. On the one hand, there was a focus among the Futurists on the pure poetic word, akin to the Suprematists' search for a painting of pure sensation. On the other hand, poetic rhythm became a weapon in the struggle against tyranny. There was to be no metrical regularity or judicious measure in the new poetic forms, since it was impossible for the poet to accommodate 'the immense soul [of the revolution], its mighty dynamism, its elemental upsurges, its fanatic and changing tempi, its zig-zags of lightning in the tiny, quietly rocking cradle of the old rhythm'.[21]

The Russian Futurists were closely allied with the Formalist critics, in what was to prove a new, highly productive liaison between literary theorists and literary practitioners. The role of

MODERNISM

the Formalists was to establish a kind of laboratory for the study of language, which would then furnish precious resources for the revolutionary writer. Rather like racing drivers, poets had a team of mechanics at their disposal who could overhaul their work. A mass study of poetic devices is essential, writes the Formalist Osip Brik, along with the laws of their historical development. What is needed, he insists, is not 'hazy little chats' about the 'proletarian spirit' and 'Communist consciousness' but clinical analysis and rigorously impersonal research.[22] The subject matter of art was no longer ideas or emotions but the material elements out of which the artwork was fashioned, organised according to specific laws and techniques. The critic was to be reinvented as technician, verbal engineer or linguistic scientist. There was to be a new science of poetic production, banishing to the outer darkness all bourgeois illusions of beauty, transcendence, creativity, inspiration and the role of the individual author. As far as the latter was concerned, one Formalist remarked that Alexander Pushkin's great poem *Eugene Onegin* (1825–32) would have been written even had Pushkin himself not existed, rather as America would have been 'discovered' had there been no Columbus.

Avant-garde experiment in the Soviet Union was not to survive the onset of Stalinism. Its counterpart in Germany was to be crushed by the Nazis, for whom all modernist art was Bolshevik art. Much of the avant-garde accordingly met its end, sabotaged not so much by internal problems as by authoritarian states. In 1930, all Soviet writers were forced by

THE DEATH OF ART

the government to join the Union of Soviet Writers, and the doctrine of socialist realism began to oust all other artistic proclivities. In the same year, Mayakovsky committed suicide.

One way in which the Dadaists closed the gap between art and life, or representation and reality, was by performance.[23] A man in a nightclub banging on a drum and screeching gibberish is not representing anything. What you are seeing is the real thing. If the Dadaists' antics were anarchic and absurd, it is because they regarded reason itself as a repressive force. Unlike the insanity of the First World War, their madness was self-conscious, and thus in their own eyes a superior form of rationality to that of the generals and politicians. Meaninglessness would become a subversive ploy. The ruling order might be accustomed to forms of sense-making hostile to its own beliefs, but the utterly fatuous was another matter. To appear on stage, as the Dadaist Hugo Ball did, with his legs sheathed in a cylinder of shiny blue cardboard so that he looked like an obelisk, was thus a political act. The audience at one Dada event was treated to a reading of obscene poetry by a young girl wearing a communion dress. At a Dada Fair in Cologne, there was a sculpture by Max Ernst with an axe attached to it so that the viewer could destroy the work if the fancy took her.[24]

The artist Marcel Duchamp famously presented a urinal as a work of art – not only to erase the boundary between art and everyday life, but also to make the point that the aesthetic is a function of its social context rather than an inherent set of

MODERNISM

features. In solemnly adding his signature to the work, he poked some satirical fun at the kind of personal imprint highly valued by the art market. Arthur Cravan, a nephew of Oscar Wilde and an associate of Dada who described himself among other things as a hotel thief, muleteer, snake charmer and chauffeur, drunkenly stripped off his clothes at a New York Dada event and was arrested by the police. He later sailed from Mexico to Buenos Aires and was never seen again. His disappearance was perhaps not unrelated to the fact that he set out from Mexico in a rowing boat.

During one performance at the Café Voltaire in Zürich, Dadaist artists demanded the right to urinate in different colours, while the audience broke obediently into its customary howling and brawling. Dada was stridently opposed to militarism, born as it was amid the carnage of the First World War, but the pacifism of the movement was strictly confined to the political sphere. During a Paris production in 1923, a fight broke out between squabbling Dadaist factions which resulted in one artist having his arm broken and another being hurled off-stage, shattering the footlights. By the time the police managed to close the theatre, the actors' costumes were in tatters.

There were plenty of other unconventional episodes. The German Dadaist Johannes Baader, having proclaimed himself President of the Globe, disrupted the inaugural meeting of the National Assembly in Weimar and demanded that the government be handed over to the Dadaists. In a manifesto of 1919, the group called for the provision of free daily meals in Berlin's

THE DEATH OF ART

Potsdamer Platz for all artists and intellectuals, the compulsory conversion of all clergymen to the Dadaist faith, the expropriation of private property, the introduction of an unintelligible poem as the official state prayer, the establishment of a Dadaist Central Office of Sexual Affairs to administer sexual relationships and the remodelling of life along Dadaist lines in every city with over fifty thousand inhabitants. Some of this was meant as a parody of other avant-gardist proclamations, while some of it (the abolition of private property, for example) was undoubtedly in earnest. The distinctions between art and kitsch, as well as between artist and spectator, were to be eradicated.

For all their anarchist leanings, a number of German Dadaists joined the German Communist Party. There were both Marxist and anarcho-communist Dadaists in Berlin in the wake of the First World War. Some members of the movement were simply cultural saboteurs, fearful that any positive political programme would quickly fall victim to the despotism of reason, while others fought for a new social order in which what was currently dismissed as nonsense might become common sense. Both they and the Surrealists who came in their wake were vehemently anti-nationalist, as well as deeply sceptical of science, rationalism, progress and technology, though some Dadaists were ambiguously allured by the machine. It was a convenient way of opposing what they saw as the bogus spirituality of the Expressionists, by whom some of them had been influenced. Despite a mystical strain, Dadaists were also allergic to orthodox religion, and took to photographing

MODERNISM

themselves insulting priests on the street. Many among their ranks were former Catholics. Beneath the carnivalesque humour and intellectual buffoonery of Dada lay a post-Nietzschean vision of the world as a seething cauldron of diffuse energies, of which humanity itself was simply a minor constituent. Denouncing what they saw as the arrogant anthropocentrism of traditional humanism, they veered from the nihilistic to the exuberant, from corrosive cynicism to spontaneous joie de vivre. If they were disgusted by humanity, which had just plunged the globe into military catastrophe, they were nonetheless champions of that momentous modernist abstraction known as Life.

Unlike the Futurists and Constructivists, Surrealism kept its distance from modern technology. As Peter Wollen points out, the movement was about 'aestheticising life rather than productivising art'.[25] Even so, the productivist artist could be seen as prefiguring a new, highly skilled form of worker, more technician than labourer, for whom work had become less fatiguing and more fulfilling. In that sense, art as production was also relevant to a more creative daily existence. Unlike the products of the Soviet avant-gardes, Surrealist art was not for the most part explicitly engagé. Its purpose was rather to expand the possibilities of consciousness in a way analogous to revolutionary action. One way to accomplish this task was by breaking down the barriers between dreaming and waking life in the name of a higher 'surreality'. In exploring heightened states of sensation and perception, its aim, as Walter Benjamin puts it,

THE DEATH OF ART

was 'to win the energies of intoxication for the revolution'.[26] Surrealism's project was to foster a revolution of everyday life, finding its home not so much in art as in the city streets. If high modernism turned its back on an alienated everyday existence, and the Constructivists and their colleagues were bent on transforming that sphere beyond recognition, the Surrealists represent a third possibility, namely to search out the inner mystery of the inconspicuous. It is a motif they inherit from both Baudelaire and Romanticism, and which can also be found in the urban landscapes of Dorothy Richardson.

The movement was fascinated by the secret life of everyday objects, as well as by the manifold ways in which the commonplace provides an entry point into the extraordinary. For those who could tap into the energies of the unconscious, the dream world was not to be seen as distinct from or superior to everyday reality, but inscribed in its every fold and crevice. As with the Russian Formalists, true perception in an alienated world involved some hard psychological, linguistic and imaginative labour. Humdrum objects could be lit up from estranging angles in a moment of what Walter Benjamin calls 'profane illumination',[27] or blasted out of their habitual contexts and violently juxtaposed with other such deracinated odds and ends. In a rebuttal of the distinction between high and popular culture, it was on the cultural detritus of daily existence – a cigarette butt, a chipped jug glimpsed for a few seconds in a second-hand store – that the salvage operations of the Surrealist imagination typically went to work.

MODERNISM

More visionary and affirmative than Dada, as well as more utopian, humanistic and theoretically minded, Surrealism was to become the most widespread and long-lasting of all the avant-garde currents, yoking Marx and Freud together in heterodox fashion and finding in the Freudian unconscious a secularised form of transcendence. (There were, to be sure, some infamous exceptions to its left-wing politics: the Surrealist painter Salvador Dalí harboured both fascist and monarchist sentiments in the 1930s.) Committed to the principles of Marxism-Leninism, the Surrealists were for the most part vehemently anti-Stalinist, denounced the dogmatism and bureaucratisation of the French Communist Party, along with its dearth of imagination, and rejected the concepts of proletarian art and socialist realism. The so-called pope of the movement, the French poet André Breton, declared that all people had the right not only to bread but to poetry.

Breton romanticised the unconscious mind, and along with his colleague Paul Éluard tried to simulate in himself states of psychosis. In Dalí's case this would almost certainly have been unnecessary. In naively libertarian fashion, the fertile resources of the unconscious were to be set free from the shackles of logic and rationality. Breton was thus among the first of a heretical band of Freudo-Marxists, a group which included Wilhelm Reich, Erich Fromm and Herbert Marcuse, and which was regarded with distinct unease by the French Communist Party of which he was a member. No doubt the party found his autocratic personality as uncongenial as his

THE DEATH OF ART

artistic views. Stalinist bureaucrats were not especially enamoured of a movement which insisted on the sovereignty of (male) desire, along with a consuming interest in dreams, sadism, alchemy, erotic fantasies, criminals, cross-dressing, sexual fetishism and the junk and rubble of everyday life. Even so, the Surrealists rallied strongly to the anti-fascist cause in France, as well as calling for an end to families, prisons, religions, armies and nations. They also championed the cause of various female assassins, including two Parisian maids who had murdered their brutal employers and a teenage prostitute who had poisoned her dissolute father.

As a penalty for his ideological aberrations, Breton was assigned to a party cell consisting of gas workers, and was instructed to report on the social and economic condition of Mussolini's Italy. Unsurprisingly, he refused this sordidly unpoetic task. He eventually became a Trotskyist, agitated against French colonialism in Africa and the Caribbean, and in partnership with Leon Trotsky produced the slogan 'The independence of art – for the revolution. The revolution – for the independence of art.' Against the left-utilitarianism of the Soviet avant-garde, art was to be both political and autonomous. In achieving for the inner life the kind of emancipation which socialism sought for the public sphere, Surrealism championed both cultural and political revolution without conflating the two. It was by remaining true to itself that art could best serve the revolution.

4

CONSERVATIVE REVOLUTIONARIES

Disputes over whether the avant-garde is part of modernism in general, or whether it represents a distinct, even adversarial current, should not delay us unduly. In the discussion that follows, I shall be drawing some distinctions between modernism and avant-gardism; but if there are vital differences between the two, there is also an abundance of overlap. It is not hard, for example, to see the avant-garde as a more militant, activist version of modernism, at times more flamboyant and at other times more austere. If some strains of modernism pare the artwork down to almost nothing, some of the avant-garde press this to the point where it may disappear altogether into its social functions. Even so, not all avant-gardism sets its face against the autonomy of the artwork, as we have seen already in the case of Surrealism. The same is true of some aspects of Dada and Futurism.

In any case, poets or dramatists who want to abolish art are not best advised to read their poetry through megaphones in

MODERNISM

factory yards, or to hand out rifles at the end of a play. They should simply stop writing. Similarly, an author who truly despairs of language stops being an author. If you liquidate the very category of the aesthetic by seeking to dissolve art into everyday life, then for better or worse you are no longer an artist, avant-garde or otherwise. It is a price some avant-gardists were prepared to pay. There were those among them for whom revolutionary art was a contradiction in terms, at least if one thought of the artwork in the manner of Immanuel Kant and his disciples as autonomous, beautiful, unified, non-practical, non-cognitive, the product of individual genius and an object of disinterested contemplation. This, by and large, is the aesthetic doctrine of Kant's *Critique of Judgement* (1790). The mistake of these avant-gardists was to assume that if one ditches this highly particular notion of art one renounces art itself, which is to pay too great a compliment to Kant.

There is, in fact, no clear-cut opposition between art as purposive and art as an end in itself. If works of art refine our sensibilities and cultivate our moral sense, is this a functional matter or not? Miracle plays, the sermons of John Donne and the political pamphlets of Jonathan Swift all have a purpose, but they can also be aesthetically enjoyable. Conversely, for art to lack a function may prove socially useful. It may enhance a political regime's reputation for it to refuse to press art into its service. During the Cold War, the CIA sponsored a travelling exhibition in Europe of American Abstract Expressionism, as a form of propaganda for the free world. The paintings' lack of

CONSERVATIVE REVOLUTIONARIES

overt political content was meant to testify to the superiority of Western civilisation over a Soviet Union for which culture was a blunt instrument of power. If the work of art is purely disinterested, as Kant and his disciples insist, it must refrain from intervening in social and political affairs; but not to act may prove as consequential as constant intervention. Refusing to challenge the prevailing social order may prove just as partisan as clamouring for its downfall. Besides, disinterestedness can be co-opted by the left as well as the right. Friedrich Schiller argues in his *On the Aesthetic Education of Man* (1794) that the work of art's refusal of one-sided commitments may allow us a foretaste of a human wholeness and harmony which has yet to be politically realised. In this sense, art's very non-political nature becomes a form of utopian politics. It bears witness to the fact that there is a life beyond the sphere of utility.

There are differences as well as affinities between modernist elites and political avant-gardes. Modernist coteries like the Bloomsbury Group, however admirably enlightened in some of their views, tend to claim a certain spiritual superiority to the philistine masses. An avant-garde, by contrast, is distinguished from the common people by forging a path which the people themselves may eventually come to tread. As the military metaphor suggests, they constitute a band of pioneers in advance of the army, and are in this sense distinct from it, but their task is to scout and skirmish on its behalf. They must clear a road for others rather than plough their own furrow. The elite is 'vertically' distinct from its less emancipated fellow

157

MODERNISM

citizens, while the vanguard is 'horizontally' so. Even so, vanguards can easily slide into elites, while the most effective elites are those aware that in order to survive they must establish a benign relationship with their social subordinates. For W.B. Yeats, the aristocrat has an intuitive understanding of the unlettered peasantry. One should treat those beneath you benevolently, thus engaging their loyalty and even their affections. It is by securing the allegiance of the masses that fascist dictators flourish.

The contrast between Stephen Dedalus and Leopold Bloom in Joyce's *Ulysses* is among things one between high modernist and avant-gardist. 'Avant-garde' may seem an eccentric description of Bloom, the small-time advertising agent; but advertising, too, blurs the distinction between art and everyday life, and Bloom's urbanised, streetwise, fragmented consciousness marks a contrast with Stephen's high modernist spiritual brooding. For Stephen, value in a ignoble modern world can be found only in the interior of the human subject. However anguished and atomised it may be, the self forms a bulwark against a social order in which everything can be measured and manipulated. Subjectivity alone is irreducible and unquantifiable. Bloom's sense of self, by contrast, is a thoroughly pragmatic affair, a mode of awareness turned outwards in a self-forgetful dialogue with his city surroundings.

Generally speaking, modernism is cosmopolitan while the avant-garde is internationalist. If the modernist artist is a citizen of the world, the avant-gardist is a citizen of a new world.

158

CONSERVATIVE REVOLUTIONARIES

The former is adrift with a bunch of fellow bohemians in the bars and cafes of some polyglot European capital, contemptuous of rhyme, iambic pentameter, the nation state and the middle-class suburb. Some avant-garde artists, by contrast, glimpse the seeds of a new global order in the world of imperialism and monopoly capitalism, and look to a solidarity among the working people of different nations. Both figures are exiles, but the avant-gardist, so to speak, is an exile from the future. Both seem to be forever on the hoof, some of them changing countries (as Brecht remarks) more often than their shoes, shifting from one metropolis, art form, journal, coterie or political current to another, forging fresh alliances and antagonising old comrades in the process. All of these drifters and expatriates belonged to the new world of international capitalism, however much some of them may have railed against the fact. Disinherited by their own cultures, rebels within their native lands, it seemed as easy to be a stranger abroad as at home. Perhaps the only way of being at home was to live in a city like Paris, where most of your colleagues were émigrés as well. Gertrude Stein, the granddaughter of German Jewish immigrants to the United States, grew up with parents who felt equally at home in America and Europe. Having lived for a while in Vienna as a small child, she chose to settle in Paris, where despite being American, Jewish, lesbian, exotically unconventional and not always the most congenial of characters, she ran the most celebrated literary salon in the city. H.D. was born in Pennsylvania but for most of her adult life she moved between London and Paris. She also spent time in Greece, Switzerland, Italy, Germany, Egypt, California and Austria, where she was psychoanalysed by Sigmund Freud. Wyndham Lewis, as though aware of this modernist mobility while still a foetus, was born on a yacht in Nova Scotia to an American mother and a British father with a Welsh surname.

In the emergent world of international capitalism, anywhere could seem interchangeable with anywhere else. In Joyce's fiction, a small, stagnant colonial capital can become the hub of the universe. Modernism, colonialism and global capitalism break up space and time, juxtaposing cultures and epochs otherwise remote from one another. In an age in which homelessness is a common situation, not least because of the upheavals of revolution and imperialist warfare, it seemed possible to turn one's lack of roots into a universal truth. The artist is representative of the human condition – but representative of it in his very isolation, central precisely because of his marginality. In a world in which everyone seems adrift, the émigré becomes typical of humanity itself.

It is remarkable how many modernist artists found themselves uprooted in this way. In their own more privileged style, they re-enacted the great tidal displacements of peoples characteristic of their time. From Oscar Wilde to V.S. Naipaul, there were those who consciously adopted a new country and culture, and in doing so could seem more native to it than those who were born and brought up there. It is thus that the phrase *plus anglais que les anglais* was coined. T.S. Eliot remarked of his American compatriot Henry James that he was a European in the way that only a non-European could be. The same might be said of Eliot himself, as he was surely aware. Some decades later, a Czech refugee renamed Tom Stoppard would demonstrate his affection for England by dining with Margaret Thatcher and engaging in a spot of grouse shooting on landed estates. The Indian author Salman Rushdie journeyed from an English public school to receiving a knighthood from Buckingham Palace.

The life of Katherine Mansfield is exemplary in this respect. Born in New Zealand, the daughter of a wealthy banker and genteel mother, she changed her name and fled from her native country in order to become a writer in England. The novelist Anthony Trollope commented on the New Zealander's 'confidence that England is the best place in the world and he is more English than any Englishman'.[1] Mansfield had visited London as a child, and spent some time later in Paris and Brussels. She identified strongly with European culture and was something of an internal exile in New Zealand, distanced from the common life of the country by her conspicuously privileged background. Yet though she was to become a valued member of the Bloomsbury Group in London, marrying John Middleton Murry and associating with Bertrand Russell, D.H. Lawrence, Lady Ottoline Morrell and a number of other cultural luminaries, she always retained a certain colonial unease in her relationship with what was then known as the mother country. If she was a habitué of English civilisation,

MODERNISM

she was also a stranger looking in from the outside, never quite at home but always on the hoof, dogged by a sense of impermanence and estrangement.

One could also turn one's expatriation to advantage by moving like Joseph Conrad among a diversity of forms of life in ways which were harder for native British artists. National cultures, so it was felt, were increasingly exhausted, a view common to both global capitalism and international socialism. Convinced that a world beyond nationhood was straining to be born, the more forward-looking writers, painters and composers of the time were not to know that the most virulent strain of nationalism of the modern age was already incubating at the heart of Europe. The nation state, it would transpire, was far from being consigned to the dust heap of history.

As aliens in both their native and adopted countries, some modernists sought to discover an alternative form of community in the cosmopolitan language of art. Perhaps the lingua franca of music, painting or sculpture might compensate for the miseries of exile – though writers, tied by their medium to a national language, are more restricted in this respect. Even *Finnegans Wake* is written in a strange species of English. Amid the babble of foreign tongues and technical idioms, art itself might constitute the only surviving meta-language, the Latin of the modern era. A temporary dwelling place might be found in an artistic movement, but such groups were notoriously fractious and sectarian, not least because of the precarious identity of their members. Behind the plight of the émigré

CONSERVATIVE REVOLUTIONARIES

lurks the modernist concern with structures, myths and archetypes, all of which promise to cut below the accidents of local and national cultures to a universal bedrock or collective unconscious. Contents may be variable, but forms remain constant. If you do not share an actual way of life with others, you might still be able to commune with them at the level of mythological fables, the discourse of the body or the grammar of the unconscious. There is a reification of form and structure – one, ironically, which reflects features of the modern world which some modernist artists find particularly unappealing.

Kinship, tradition, citizenship, political allegiance and sexual reproduction are bonds which exist to be broken, as with the aloof, sardonic figure of Joyce's Stephen Dedalus, a parody of the alienated modernist artist. Rather as the autonomous work of art rejects all dependence on its surroundings, so the artist himself is gripped by the Oedipal fantasy of being self-born. Freedom consists in breaking away, as Ibsen's Nora Helmer of *A Doll's House* (1879) bravely abandons her home and husband. For others, even to imagine a new form of life, as with the disenchanted Rupert Birkin of Lawrence's *Women in Love*, is to be held hostage by the language of the present. Romanticism, too, knows the ache of dispossession; but whereas some of its poets and philosophers are in pursuit of a spiritual homeland, modernism is inclined to embrace homelessness as a staple feature of the human condition. That desire knows no natural closure is a tenet of the eminently modernist discourse of psychoanalysis.

163

MODERNISM

When asked what he thought went to make up modern culture, T.S. Eliot replied, 'Byzantine, Polynesian, African, Hebridean [and] Chinese . . . art'.[2] No doubt there is a touch of mandarin mischief about this response, but there is some truth in it as well. Modernism, writes Edward Said, is among other things a matter of 'massive infusions of non-European cultures into the metropolitan heartland during the early years of this century'.[3] There was a good deal of cultish 'Orientalism' and off-the-peg Eastern spirituality about the movement, as what was felt to be a jaded Western rationality sought to reinvigorate itself by tapping into some arcane sources of energy. The infusion was to repeat itself in a more minor key in the late 1960s. Yet as Said points out, there was also a busy traffic of artists and students across the globe, as traditional frontiers were breached, new cultural journals and associations sprang up and African, Indian, Caribbean, Vietnamese and other so-called Third World intellectuals flocked to Paris and London. If modernism pitches the most heterogeneous materials together, so do colonialism and imperialism.

The influence of non-European civilisations on modernism is among its most striking features, not least if one contrasts it with the more parochial art of realism. At the same time, one must beware of celebrating the exilic and transgressive as virtues in themselves, as some (post)modernist writing tends rashly to do. If some modernist artists treated borders and nation states with disdain, so does Coca-Cola and sex trafficking.

CONSERVATIVE REVOLUTIONARIES

Boundaries can be protective as well as restrictive. There are even ways in which the nation state can provide a degree of shelter from the predatory world of global capitalism. One should also recall that the nation state was a revolutionary conception in its time, and that – as some of the great empires of modern history have discovered to their cost – there are emancipatory as well as oppressive forms of nationalism.

When it comes to the politics of modernism, the avant-garde can usually be found on the political left, while an embarrassingly large number of modernists adhere to the political right. Yet the contrast is far from absolute. We have seen already that there were avant-gardists on the extreme right (Italian Futurism), while some modernists of a non-avant-garde stripe were political radicals or even revolutionaries. Mallarmé had anarchist sympathies, Rimbaud was a ferocious political rebel, some of the Neo-Impressionists were political leftists, Oscar Wilde was an Irish republican socialist, while the young James Joyce cherished similar convictions before evolving later into a liberal or social democrat. Samuel Beckett was an actual rather than metaphorical guerrilla fighter against fascism. In *A Room of One's Own* (1929), Virginia Woolf presented the world with one of the most subversive non-fictional documents in the English literary canon. Not a few modernist writers either joined or fellow-travelled with European communist parties. If there is Marinetti, there is also Mayakovsky. Bertolt Brecht and Seán O'Casey were on the Marxist left, while the Italian poet

165

MODERNISM

Gabriele D'Annunzio, along with the German writers Gottfried Benn and Ernst Jünger, were ensconced on the far right.

There were Nazi-sympathising Expressionists, but also communist-leaning ones. The latter group included a trio of left-wing Liverpudlian-Irish seamen who published Expressionist fiction in the 1920s and 1930s.[4] Martin Heidegger might justly be regarded as *the* philosopher of modernism, with his spiritual elitism, far right-wing political sympathies, nostalgia for the presence of the gods and patrician distaste for the mass and mechanical. In his hostility to science, technology, rationalism, democracy, bureaucracy, materialism and liberal values, one can find reflected a sizeable swathe of modernist biases. Yet there is also the Vienna philosophical circle, which was far more enlightened in its social values, and which was forced into exile by the advent of Hitler. If the political theory of the age has its Carl Schmitt, philosopher of Nazism, it can also boast of Antonio Gramsci.

Mixed though it is, however, the political record of modernism as a whole is fairly dire. Conrad was a deep-dyed conservative and misogynist with a virulent hatred of the political left. Ezra Pound and Wyndham Lewis supported the fascist cause, while Yeats, a champion of aristocracy, elitism and political violence, flirted with fascism as well. Like the German poet Gottfried Benn, he also advocated eugenics as a way of preventing the 'lower orders' from breeding. The heroine of Dorothy Richardson's *Pilgrimage* has moments of visceral anti-Semitism which seem not far removed from the views of

CONSERVATIVE REVOLUTIONARIES

her creator. Richardson herself betrayed the prejudices of her genteel background by describing D.H. Lawrence as 'a surly artisan scowling'.[5] T.S. Eliot, who as we have seen was tainted by anti-Semitism, was a royalist and high Tory who at one stage lent his support to a quasi-fascistic French organisation. Lawrence's largely reactionary politics we have noted already. Gertrude Stein supported the pro-Nazi Vichy regime in the Second World War, disdained all partisan politics even when Hitler was on the march throughout Europe and was more of a misogynist than a feminist.

Marianne Moore, by contrast, was a socialist as a student and later a liberal apologist for civic and individual freedom, chiding Ireland for its neutral stance during the Second World War and praising Denmark for giving sanctuary to Jews. She was an ardent advocate of non-violence, though she supported the United States' war against Vietnam and preferred the reign of Lyndon Johnson to the administration of John F. Kennedy. She also wrote poetry about the war, a rare political intervention among modernist poets, and spoke out against racism in the US. None of these authors except Stein and Moore were in any significant sense a democrat. Joyce, an erstwhile socialist, is another exception to this unsavoury crew, as is the path-breaking feminist Virginia Woolf, despite her odiously snobbish remarks about her Irish colleague. Joyce also stands out from his melancholic fellow modernists in his profoundly comic vision of the world, in both the everyday and Dantesque senses of the word.

MODERNISM

If a good deal of modernism was infected by extreme right-wing views, it is partly because the thinker who shaped so much of it was a strident spokesman for the political right. Friedrich Nietzsche, who was a source of inspiration for Yeats, Lawrence and a number of other modernists, holds that God is dead, tradition is in tatters and any form of foundationalism bankrupt. Meanings and values are not given but created. Art is the supreme value, while both stable objects and unified human subjects are fictions. Language and rationality are maladroit mechanisms which chop up reality into arbitrary chunks with no basis in reality. The world is no way in particular, and truth is simply a convenient falsehood. Meaning is imposed by those who wield the most authority. Ideals and ideas are for the most part spurious rationalisations of interest, power and appetite. Everyday life is despicably mediocre, and the common people a contemptible rabble. Only the spiritual elite can acknowledge the ungrounded nature of human existence, and only the so-called Supermen among them have the courage to rejoice in this condition, laughing and dancing on the edge of the abyss. It is the bovine masses who trust blindly that they have solid ground beneath their feet, at the very moment when such metaphysical terra firma has crumbled to nothing.

History in Nietzsche's eyes is a chapter of gruesome accidents without design or direction, and reality is in ceaseless, meaningless flux. Fragmented works of art thus represent the new realism, showing us the way the world is. Those who are

CONSERVATIVE REVOLUTIONARIES

free are those who can say 'yes' to the eternal return of everything we have known, a return entirely without point or purpose. Reason must yield ground to myth, so that one thinks with the blood and the instincts rather than with anything as bungling and inept as the intellect. It is almost a programme for modernism, or at least for some influential strains of it. Much of it is also the orthodoxy of the postmodern, which in some ways can be summarised as Nietzsche without the politics. Myth provides the modernists with a source of wisdom which preceded our calamitous fall into rationalism, as with *The Waste Land*, but also with a pragmatic means of organising an amorphous everyday life, as with *Ulysses*. Yet whereas Nietzsche exults in the death of absolute truth, not least because it allows a select band of bold spirits like himself to forge their own values, modernism is for the most part plunged into mourning for it.

Nietzsche's writings represent a deep-seated crisis of rationality in late nineteenth-century Europe – a crisis of which modernism is one major inheritor. Faced with this emergency, one can take either of two routes. On the one hand, there is the path of the avant-garde, which seeks to turn the material infrastructure of capitalist society against its traditional values and institutions. Many avant-gardists appeal to speed, flux, utility, function, novelty, mechanisation and technological reason; but one reason for doing so is to undermine the middle-class faith in deep subjectivity, rooted identities, historical continuities and immutable moral doctrines. It is thus that

169

MODERNISM

technology and innovation can be drawn upon to sabotage political order and social hierarchy. There are other middle-class values to be flouted as well, such as the sacredness of the family, the uniqueness of the individual, the eternal nature of truth and the hallowed status of art. In this way, one dimension of middle-class civilisation is turned aggressively against the other. Some avant-gardists are anti-bourgeois but not anti-capitalist, scoffing at middle-class pieties while lavishing praise on the rational organisation of factory labour known as Fordism. There are also those who mistake modernisation for socialism.

The process, however, can be put into reverse. You can also celebrate subjectivity, the infinite, the imperishable value of art and the wisdom of tradition against the crass cults of mechanism, utility and instrumental reason which threaten to bring these values to ruin. In Marxist terms, you can either turn the base against the superstructure, or the superstructure against the base. Both responses tend to be drastically one-sided – either too complacent about modernity or too darkly apocalyptic.

The contradictions of modernism, then, have their source in the contradictions of capitalist society. In fact, modernism's ambiguous relation to that form of life has often been remarked. 'The various modernisms', remarks Fredric Jameson, 'have just as often constituted violent reactions against modernisation as they have replicated its values and tendencies.'[6] We have seen already that T.J. Clark speaks of modernism as being caught between horror and elation at the forces which

170

CONSERVATIVE REVOLUTIONARIES

drive modern existence forward. Yet things are not always as complex as that. By and large, modernist works are *either* horrified *or* elated by the present – violent reactions to modernity, or uncritical replications of it. For the most part, it is the avant-garde which greets the modern in effusive spirit, and non-avant-gardist artists who are inclined to be dismayed by it.

There are, to be sure, literary works which draw on distinctively modern forms of experience while taking up a largely negative attitude towards them. Eliot's poetry may serve as an example. One thinks also of the work of Pound, which is modernist in form yet critical of modernity in content. You can lament the spiritual bankruptcy of the modern age by employing techniques which that age has itself invented. Not much modernist art, however, combines a whole-hearted zest for modernity with a deep-seated revulsion from it, as some of Dickens's novels do. One of the most intriguing aspects of the great railway passage in *Dombey and Son* (1846–8) is that the author seems not to know what to think of these sinister, exhilarating new inventions, which are sombrely branded emblems of death at the very moment that the prose is electric with their futuristic promise. Dickens is quite often unsure whether to be scandalised or entertained by what he presents. He even manages to wring a few laughs out of the appalling Dotheboys Hall in *Nicholas Nickleby* (1838–9).

Though many modernist writers decry the barrenness of the age, few of them question the material interests which underlie this sterility, or suggest political solutions to it.

MODERNISM

For Yeats, Eliot, Rilke, Lawrence, Stevens, Ernst Jünger and others, radical politics is part of the problem, not part of the solution. It is simply more soulless mechanism, the latest manifestation of a modernity they abhor. Socialism means industry, democracy, technology, bureaucracy, materialism and the triumph of the benighted masses. It is every bit as inimical to the life of the spirit as the marketplace. In turning its back on a squalid modern era, then, a good deal of modernism also repudiates the political forces that might transform it. The artist, remarks Mallarmé, is on strike against society; but a strike is an act of withdrawal rather than engagement.

What are we to make of the fact that some of the finest literary work of the twentieth century stems from the reactionary end of the political spectrum? Or if not exactly from there, then from a lip-curling contempt for everyday life? It would certainly seem to question the vulgar Marxist view that bad ideology makes for bad art. In fact, one might go further and claim that it is that very ideology, obnoxious though much of it may be, that gives birth to such superlative writing. The vision of life revealed in these works is a radical one – a radicalism of the right, often enough, but no less rich and wide-ranging for that, and as much at odds with middle-class mores as the revolutionary left. Generally speaking, modernist art springs not from the social mainstream, with its faith in private property, civil rights, liberal democracy, social equality, tolerance, pluralism, rational argument, individual freedom, scientific progress and the like, but from the wilder fringes of

CONSERVATIVE REVOLUTIONARIES

European civilisation. Yet if it is more extremist than the world of E.M. Forster and Katherine Mansfield, it is also more audacious and imaginative. It poses questions which cut far deeper than the issue of personal relationships, or individual morality, or how to survive in middle-class suburbia. In this sense, it can give birth to some magnificent art partly because of its radical-right viewpoint, not in spite of it.

We have seen already that the émigré status of some modernist writers can breed in them an appetite for order and tradition. Displaced and unsettled, some of them cling to the values of hierarchy and authority more tenaciously than most insiders do. Yet their being expatriates also lends their art a synoptic range and cultural diversity denied to the likes of Arnold Bennett and Evelyn Waugh. Being personally caught up in the crisis of exile and belonging, tradition and identity typical of their time, they can register it all the more graphically in their writing. What bolsters their conservatism, then, is also what underlies their breadth and boldness of outlook.

Moreover, because artists like James, Shaw, Wilde, Conrad, Yeats, Eliot, Mansfield, Pound, Joyce, Lawrence and Beckett move among different nations, they can bring a powerfully distancing perspective to bear on them, one relatively free of the constraints of those for whom such cultures are bred in the bone. In the work of these authors, then, the very foundations of civilisation could be called into question. To be situated at once inside and outside a particular culture is rarely the most comfortable spot to inhabit; but modernism, along with some

MODERNISM

of the post-colonial writing that has followed in its wake, would suggest that it is nonetheless one of the most artistically fruitful.

Modernism represents among other things a search for an alternative kind of rationality, in an age when the prevailing versions of reason seem to have calamitously failed. A good many such conventional models lay broken and rusting on the battlefields of the First World War. It is never easy, however, to draw a firm line between a constructive critique of the ruling forms of reason on the one hand, and a potentially sinister irrationalism on the other. Feminism might be taken to exemplify the former, while fascism is an instance of the latter. The line between reason transformed and reason spurned is one that the modernists continually cross, and one with which we still have trouble today. In this sense, though modernism itself now lies over a century behind us, many of the problems it addresses are as insistent as ever.

174

NOTES

1 THE TIME OF MODERNISM

1. See Lawrence Rainey (ed.), *Modernism: An Anthology* (Oxford, 2005), p. xxi.
2. In *The Five Paradoxes of Modernity* (New York, 1990), Antoine Compagnon (or his translator, Franklin Philip) frequently uses the term 'modernity' to designate what in English would be known as 'modernism', with a number of consequent confusions. The title of the book is itself misleading in this respect.
3. Malcolm Bull, 'Between the Cultures of Capital', *New Left Review*, no. 11 (September/October 2001), p. 96.
4. For the global reach of modernism, see *The Routledge Encyclopedia of Modernism*, www.rem.routledge.com. See also Mark Wollaeger (ed.), *The Oxford Handbook of Global Modernisms* (Oxford, 2012), and Joe Cleary, *Modernism, Empire, World Literature* (Cambridge, 2021). Since I myself have little competence in the general field of (post-)colonial studies, I shall confine my comments on this subject to the one culture of this kind with which I am acquainted from the inside: Britain's oldest colony, and the first post-colonial nation of the twentieth century, Ireland.
5. Slavoj Žižek, *Absolute Recoil* (London, 2014), p. 157. I use the term 'movement', which overlooks the plurality of modernism, purely for convenience.
6. Franco Moretti, *Distant Reading* (London, 2013), pp. 35–6.

175

NOTES TO PP. 5–23

7. Perry Anderson, 'Modernity and Revolution', *New Left Review*, no. 144 (March/April 1984). For the continuing dominance of cultural tradition, see Arno Mayer, *The Persistence of the Old Regime* (New York, 1981).

8. Anderson, 'Modernity and Revolution', p. 105.

9. Anderson, 'Modernity and Revolution', pp. 106–7.

10. For an outstandingly well-informed account of such modernist tributaries, see Peter Nicholls, *Modernisms: A Literary Guide* (London, 1995).

11. Quoted by Michele Barrett and Jean Radford, 'Modernism in the 1930s: Dorothy Richardson and Virginia Woolf', in Francis Barker et al. (eds), *The Politics of Modernism* (Colchester, 1979).

12. Raymond Williams, *The Politics of Modernism*, ed. Tony Pinkney (London, 1989), p. 34.

13. I mean by 'nominalism' the claim that all that the members of a certain category share in common is their name.

14. For the latter dating, see Francis Mulhern, *Into the Mêlée: Culture/Politics/Intellectuals* (London, 2024), p. 28.

15. T.J. Clark, *Farewell to an Idea* (London, 1999), p. 15.

16. See in particular Greenberg's *Art and Culture: Critical Essays* (Boston, 1961), and Blanchot's *The Space of Literature* (Lincoln, NE, 1989).

17. For a useful account of the movement, see McKenzie Wark, *The Beach beneath the Street* (London and New York, 2011).

18. Quoted in John Willett, *The New Sobriety* (London, 1978), p. 119.

19. Joseph Conrad, *The Secret Agent* (1907), chapter 8.

20. See Frank Kermode, *The Classic: Literary Images of Permanence and Change* (London, 1975).

21. Quoted in Antoine Compagnon, *The Five Paradoxes of Modernity* (New York, 1994), p. 62.

22. Henri Bergson, *Creative Evolution* (1907; repr. New York, 1998), p. 11.

23. Hannah Arendt, *The Human Condition* (1958; repr. Chicago and London, 1998), p. 246.

24. Charles Baudelaire, *The Painter of Modern Life and Other Essays* (London, 1964), p. 10.

25. Quoted in Hugh Kenner, *The Pound Era* (London, 1991), p. 436.

26. Quoted in David Frisby, *Fragments of Modernity* (Cambridge, 1985), p. 57.

27. Edward Thomas, 'The Glory', *The Collected Poems of Edward Thomas* (Oxford, 1978), p. 199.

NOTES TO PP. 25–63

28. See his 'Theses on the Philosophy of History', in Walter Benjamin, *Illuminations*, ed. Hannah Arendt (London, 1973).
29. See Edward Timms and David Kelley (eds), *Unreal City: Urban Experience in Modern European Literature and Art* (Manchester, 1985).
30. Walter Benjamin, *One-Way Street and Other Writings* (London, 1978), p. 231.
31. Fredric Jameson, *The Modernist Papers* (London, 2007), p. 5.
32. Paul de Man, 'Literary History and Literary Modernity', in *Blindness and Insight: Essays in the Rhetoric of Contemporary Criticism* (Minneapolis, 1983), p. 162.
33. Stefan Collini, *Absent Minds* (Oxford, 2006), p. 421.
34. Peter Osborne, *The Politics of Time* (London, 1995), p. 137.
35. Fredric Jameson, *Postmodernism, or, The Culture of Late Capitalism* (London, 1991), p. 307.
36. Jameson, *Postmodernism*, p. 311.
37. Warwick Research Collective, *Combined and Uneven Development: Towards a New Theory of World Literature* (Liverpool, 2015), p. 54.
38. For the relations between modernism and imperialism, see Fredric Jameson, 'Modernism and Imperialism', in Seamus Deane, Terry Eagleton, Fredric Jameson and Edward Said, *Nationalism, Colonialism and Literature* (Minneapolis, 1990), Howard J. Booth and Nigel Rigby (eds), *Modernism and Empire* (Manchester, 2000) and Joe Cleary, *Modernism, Empire, World Literature* (Cambridge, 2021).
39. See Kristin Ross, *The Emergence of Social Space* (Minneapolis, 1988), especially chapter 1.
40. See Perry Anderson, 'Components of the National Culture', *New Left Review*, no. 50 (July/August 1968).
41. Anderson, 'Components of the National Culture', p. 113.
42. Clark, *Farewell to an Idea*, p. 3.
43. For a valuable account of the modern in these terms, see Marshall Berman, *All That Is Solid Melts into Air* (New York, 1988).

2 WORDS AND THINGS

1. Quoted by David Frisby, 'Introduction', Georg Simmel, *The Philosophy of Money* (London, 2011), pp. xxi–xxii.
2. Clark, *Farewell to an Idea*, p. 7.
3. Robert B. Pippin, *Modernism as a Philosophical Problem* (Oxford, 1999), p. 6.
4. See Raymond Williams, *The Long Revolution* (London, 1961), chapters 2 & 3.

NOTES TO PP. 63–92

5. Martin Heidegger, *Being and Time* (Oxford, 1962), p. 164.
6. Henry James, *Selected Literary Criticism*, ed. Morris Shapira (Harmondsworth, 1963), p. 181.
7. Henry James, *The House of Fiction* (London, 1957), p. 201.
8. See Linda Leavell, *Holding On Upside Down: The Life and Work of Marianne Moore* (London, 2013), p. 347.
9. Jameson, *Postmodernism*, p. 307.
10. See Lucy Daniel, *Gertrude Stein* (London, 2009), p. 58.
11. James, *Selected Literary Criticism*, p. 219.
12. James, *Selected Literary Criticism*, p. 226.
13. James, *Selected Literary Criticism*, p. 221.
14. James, *Selected Literary Criticism*, p. 218.
15. James, *Selected Literary Criticism*, p. 226.
16. James, *Selected Literary Criticism*, p. 224.
17. Quoted in Chris Pike (ed.), *The Futurists, the Formalists and the Marxist Critique* (London, 1979), p.13.
18. T.E. Hulme, *Further Speculations* (Minneapolis, 1955), p. 10.
19. Bertolt Brecht, *Brecht on Theatre: The Development of an Aesthetic*, ed. and trans. John Willett (New York, 1964).
20. James, *Selected Literary Criticism*, p. 85.
21. Hugo von Hofmannsthal, *The Lord Chandos Letter and Other Writings* (New York, 2005), pp. 121–2.
22. Malcolm Bull, *Anti-Nietzsche* (London, 2011), p. 127.
23. Hofmannsthal, *The Lord Chandos Letter*, p. 123.
24. Hofmannsthal, *The Lord Chandos Letter*, pp. 127–8.
25. Fredric Jameson, *The Modernist Papers* (London, 2007), pp. 140, 160.
26. Hofmannsthal, *The Lord Chandos Letter*, p. 120.
27. Hofmannsthal, *The Lord Chandos Letter*, p. 125.
28. Quoted in Daniel, *Gertrude Stein*, p. 32.
29. For a useful account, see Michael Sherringham, *Everyday Life: Theories and Practices from Surrealism to the Present* (Oxford, 2006).
30. Gershom Scholem, *Walter Benjamin: The Story of a Friendship* (London, 1982), p. 59 (italics in original).
31. Quoted in Williams, *The Politics of Modernism*, p. 73.
32. Quoted in David Hopkins, *Dada and Surrealism: A Very Short Introduction* (Oxford, 2004), pp. 31–2.
33. See Luke Gibbons, *James Joyce and the Irish Revolution* (Chicago, 2023), p. 102.
34. Quoted in Jean Radford, *Dorothy Richardson* (Hemel Hempstead, 1991), p. 3.

NOTES TO PP. 92–109

35. Henry James, *The Wings of the Dove* (1902), Book 10.
36. Virginia Woolf, *To the Lighthouse* (1927).
37. Stéphane Mallarmé, *Selected Prose, Poems, Essays and Letters* (Baltimore, 1956), p. 38.
38. One of the finest theorists of the crisis of language in the modernist era is the Austrian satirist Karl Kraus. See *In These Great Times: A Karl Kraus Reader* (Manchester, 1984).
39. Jacques Rancière, *The Politics of Literature* (Cambridge, 2011), p. 5.
40. Quoted in Jameson, *The Modernist Papers*, p. xx.
41. Luigi Russolo, 'The Art of Noises: A Futurist Manifesto', quoted in Lawrence Rainey (ed.), *Modernism: An Anthology* (Oxford, 2005), p. 24.
42. Jacques Derrida, *Writing and Difference* (Chicago, 1978), p. 240.
43. See *Selected Writings of Gertrude Stein* (New York, 1990), p. 249.
44. Walter Benjamin, 'Surrealism', in *One-Way Street and Other Writings*, p. 226.
45. Quoted in Kenner, *The Pound Era*, p. 185.
46. For the Russian Formalists, see Victor Erlich, *Russian Formalism: History and Doctrine* (The Hague, 1955), Stephen Bann and John E. Bowlt (eds), *Russian Formalism* (Edinburgh, 1973) and Tony Bennett, *Formalism and Marxism* (London, 1979).
47. Viktor Shklovsky, 'Revolution of the Word', in *Viktor Shklovsky: A Reader*, ed. and trans. Alexandra Berlin (New York, 2016).
48. Gertrude Stein, *Four in America* (New Haven, 1947), p. vi.
49. Quoted in Christina Lodder, *Russian Constructivism* (New Haven and London, 1983), p. 77.
50. See Terry Eagleton, *Critical Revolutionaries* (London, 2022), chapter 4.
51. Quoted in Charles Taylor, *Sources of the Self* (Cambridge, 1989), p. 484.
52. Quoted in Pike (ed.), *The Futurists, the Formalists and the Marxist Critique*, p. 194.
53. For a valuable collection of essays on modernism and gender, see Bonnie Kime Scott (ed.), *The Gender of Modernism* (Bloomington and Indianapolis, 1990).
54. I have been rapped over the knuckles for a previous expression of this view by Stefan Collini, who like many an English intellectual seems to imagine that any positive commentary on Ireland by one of his compatriots is bound to be disreputably sentimental. See Collini's *Absent Minds: Intellectuals in Britain* (Oxford, 2006), p. 191. One who has lived in Ireland for many years is unlikely to romanticise the place.

NOTES TO PP. 115–134

55. 'The Critic as Artist', in *The Works of Oscar Wilde*, ed. G.F. Maine (London, 1949), p. 963.
56. See Matei Calinescu, *Five Faces of Modernity* (Durham, NC, 1987), p. 45.
57. See in particular his *Aesthetic Theory* (London, 1984).
58. Theodor Adorno, *Prisms* (London, 1967), p. 32.
59. Theodor Adorno, 'Commitment', in E. Bloch et al., *Aesthetics and Politics* (London, 1977), p. 180.
60. Tom F. Driver, 'Beckett by the Madeleine,' interview, *Columbia University Forum*, IV (Summer 1961), p. 23.
61. Compare, for example, a six-month-old infant with a sixty-year-old adult.

3 THE DEATH OF ART

1. See C.D. Innes, *Erwin Piscator's Political Theatre* (Cambridge, 1972).
2. Innes, *Erwin Piscator's Political Theatre*, p. 54.
3. For an excellent account of the various European avant-gardes, see John Willett, *The Age of Sobriety: Art and Politics in the Weimar Republic, 1917–1933* (London, 1978). See also Pike (ed.), *The Futurists, the Formalists and the Marxist Critique*, and Christina Lodder, *Russian Constructivism* (New Haven and London, 1982).
4. A similar political animus against the avant-garde is evident in Calinescu, *The Five Faces of Modernity*.
5. See Renato Poggioli, *The Theory of the Avant-Garde* (Cambridge, MA, 1968).
6. Peter Bürger, *Theory of the Avant-Garde* (Minneapolis, 1984), p. 20.
7. Clark, *Farewell to an Idea*, p. 8.
8. See Berman, *All That Is Solid Melts into Air*.
9. Anderson, 'Modernity and Revolution', p. 98.
10. Quoted in Rainey (ed.), *Modernism: An Anthology*, pp. 4–5.
11. Though the relationship between Futurism and fascism is a complex one. See Judy Davies, 'Marinetti and the Fascists of Milan', in Edward Timms and Peter Collier (eds), *Visions and Blueprints: Avant-Garde Culture and Radical Politics in Early Twentieth-Century Europe* (Manchester, 1988).
12. See Lodder, *Russian Constructivism*, p. 201.
13. Quoted in Lodder, *Russian Constructivism*, p. 48. The Dutch avant-garde movement De Stijl, while less politically militant than the Russian Constructivists, shared some of their aims. See Elsa Strietman, 'De Stijl: Style and Idea', in Timms and Collier (eds), *Visions and Blueprints*.

180

NOTES TO PP. 135–170

14. Nikolai Punin, quoted in Lodder, *Russian Constructivism*, p. 56.
15. Quoted in Lodder, *Russian Constructivism*, p. 121.
16. Simone Weil, 'The Human Personality', in Sian Miles (ed.), *Simone Weil: An Anthology* (London, 2005), p. 74.
17. I have developed these ideas more fully in my book *The English Novel: An Introduction* (Oxford, 2005), chapter 12.
18. B. Arvatov, 'Utopia or Science?', quoted in Lodder, *Russian Constructivism*, p. 278.
19. Quoted in Lodder, *Russian Constructivism*, p. 24.
20. Nicholas Gorlov, 'Futurism and Revolution', quoted in Pike (ed.), *The Futurists, the Formalists and the Marxist Critique*, p. 200.
21. Gorlov, quoted in Pike (ed.), *The Futurists, the Formalists and the Marxist Critique*, p. 211.
22. O.M. Brik, 'The So-Called "Formal Method"', in *Screen Reader: Cinema/Ideology/Politics* (London, 1977), p. 275.
23. I am much indebted in what follows to Hopkins, *Dada and Surrealism*. A classic scholarly work on Surrealism is Maurice Nadeau's *The History of Surrealism* (Harmondsworth, 1973). For other useful studies, see Anna Balakian, *Surrealism: The Road to the Absolute* (London, 1972). There is a valuable commentary on Dada in Richard Sheppard's remarkably erudite, wide-ranging study *Modernism – Dada – Postmodernism* (Evanston, IL, 2000), chapters 7–13.
24. See Hopkins, *Dada and Surrealism*, p. 33.
25. Peter Wollen, 'The Situationist International', *New Left Review*, no. 174 (March/April 1989), p. 79.
26. Benjamin, *One-Way Street*, p. 236.
27. Benjamin, *One-Way Street*, p. 227.

4 CONSERVATIVE REVOLUTIONARIES

1. Quoted in Claire Tomalin, *Katherine Mansfield: A Secret Life* (London, 1987), p. 8.
2. Quoted in Peter Childs, *Modernism* (London, 2008), p. 35.
3. Edward Said, *Culture and Imperialism* (London, 1993), p. 292.
4. The three authors were George Garrett, James Hanley and Jim Phelan. See Ken Worpole, 'Expressionism and Working-Class Fiction', *New Left Review*, no. 130 (November/December 1981).
5. Quoted in Gloria Fromm, *Dorothy Richardson: A Biography* (Urbana, IL, 1977), p. 232.
6. Jameson, *Postmodernism*, p. 304.

INDEX

Abstract Expressionism, 7, 156
abstraction, 104–5
Adorno, Theodor, 116–18
aestheticism, 14, 111
agitprop theatre groups, 122, 134
Amis, Kingsley, 13
Anderson, Perry, 5, 49, 50, 54, 130
Arendt, Hannah, 21
Artaud, Antonin, 86, 98
autonomy, and art, 107–14
avant-garde, and modernism, 125–47, 155–9

Baader, Johannes, 148
Bakhtin, Mikhail, 86
Ball, Hugo, 35, 88–9, 147
Barthes, Roland, 86, 97
Baudelaire, Charles, 21–2, 61, 75, 126
Bauhaus, 18–19, 133
Beardsley, Aubrey, 47
Becher, J.R., *Workers, Peasants, Soldiers*, 124

Beckett, Samuel, 11, 14, 50, 87–8, 97, 113–14, 118, 165
Benjamin, Walter, 25–6, 40, 43, 99, 150–1, 151
Benn, Gottfried, 166
Bergson, Henri, *Creative Evolution* (1907), 20, 90
Berman, Marshall, 129–30
Blake, William, 114
Blanchot, Maurice, 15
Bloomsbury Group, 157, 161
Borges, Jorge Luis, 128
Brecht, Bertholt: and the avant-garde, 125, 133, 159; on drama, 75; epic theatre of, 128; and Marxism, 165; and method acting, 138; in the Weimar Republic, 123
Breton, André, 152–3
Brik, Osip, 146
British traditionalism, 46–9
Büchner, Georg, *Woyzeck*, 16

INDEX

Bull, Malcolm, 2, 78
Bürger, Peter, 126–7

Camus, Albert, 97–8
Celan, Paul, 97
Chaplin, Charlie, 26
CIA, American Abstract Expressionism exhibition, 156–7
cinema, and the avant-garde, 125
Clark, T.J., 13–14, 54, 60, 129, 170
Cohen, Joshua, *The Netanyahus*, 21
Collini, Stefan, 38, 179n54
Compagnon, Antoine, *The Five Paradoxes of Modernity*, 126, 175n2
Conrad, Joseph, 11, 48, 67, 162, 166; *Heart of Darkness*, 42, 46; *Nostromo*, 29; *The Secret Agent*, 19–20, 31–7
Constructivists, 71, 101, 103, 122, 125, 133–8, 143
craft, 143
Cravan, Arthur, 148
Cubists, 87, 101, 118, 122, 125, 137

Dadaists, 5, 26, 34–5, 64, 71, 87, 101, 134, 147–50
Daily Mail (newspaper), 63
Dalí, Salvador, 152
D'Annunzio, Gabriele, 166
David, Jacques-Louis, 13–14
De Man, Paul, 37–8
De Stijl (avant-garde movement), 180n13
Defoe, Daniel, 48
dehumanisation, and the avant-garde, 138

Deleuze, Gilles, 21
Derrida, Jacques, 98
Descartes, René, 140
Dickens, Charles, 55, 91–2, 109, 171
Dix, Otto, 123
Duchamp, Marcel, 147–8

Edgeworth, Maria, 50–1
Einstein, Albert, 26
Eisentein, Sergei, 91–2, 121, 133, 134
Eisler, Hanns, 123
Eliot, T.S.: drawn to England, 48; fondness for jazz and music hall, 87; on Henry James, 160–1; and the impersonal, 139; on the inarticulacy of language, 24; and the Metaphysical poets, 119; negativity, 171; and non-European cultures, 164; and politics, 167, 172; and symbolism, 84–5; 'A Cooking Egg' (1917), 81–3; *Four Quartets*, 11, 17, 79; 'Gerontion' (1920), 83; 'Tradition and the Individual Talent,' 41, 140; *The Waste Land*, 11, 12, 30, 41, 66, 97, 129, 169
Éluard, Paul, 152
English Workers' Theatre Movement, 122
ennui, 87
Ernst, Max, 147
estrangement, 71, 102–3
everyday life, modernist treatment of, 85–8, 96–7
existentialism, 96–7
Expressionists, 98, 139, 166

183

INDEX

Fascism, 43, 174

Faulkner, William, 100; *The Sound and the Fury*, 13

film: *see* cinema

First World War, 3–4

Fitzgerald, F. Scott, *The Great Gatsby*, 42

Flaubert, Gustav, 65, 98; *Sentimental Education* (1869), 66

Fordism, 137, 170

Formalists, 71, 101–3, 118, 145–6

Forster, E.M.: *Howards End* (1910), 69; *A Passage to India*, 11, 46, 80

Freud, Sigmund, 30–1, 43, 142, 152, 160

Fromm, Erich, 152

Futurists, 27, 104, 131–4, 137, 144–5

Gautier, Théophile, 14, 115

Germany, Weimar Republic, 122–3

Goebbels, Josef, 132

Gramsci, Antonio, 166

Greenberg, Clement, 15

Gregory, Augusta, 53, 54

Gropius, Walter, 133

Grosz, George, 123

H.D. (Hilda Doolittle), 17–18, 41–2, 66, 97, 99, 159–60

Hardy, Thomas, 48, 116

Heaney, Seamus, 103

Heidegger, Martin, 9, 63, 85, 166

Heisenberg, Werner, 90

Hemingway, Ernest, 97–8

Hitchcock, Alfred, *Psycho*, 124

Hofmannsthal, Hugo von, 'The Chandos Letter' (1902), 76–81

Hopkins, Gerard Manley, 73, 100, 114

Hulme, T.E., 72–3

Ibsen, Henrik, 11, 30; *A Doll's House* (1879), 163

Imagists, 17–18, 98, 99, 100, 103

impersonality, 139–42

internationalism, 158–63

Ireland, Great Famine, 49–50, 52

Irish language, 52

Irish modernism, 49–54

James, Henry: disregard for subject matter, 65–6; drawn to England, 48; European consciousness, 161; on experience as sensibility, 76; on Flaubert, 98; prose style, 92–3, 99; *The Ambassadors*, 57; 'The Art of Fiction' (1888), 69; 'The Future of the Novel' (1900), 66, 69–71; 'Greville Fane' (1892), 113; 'The Turn of the Screw' (1898), 11

Jameson, Fredric, 27–8, 44, 68, 78–9, 170

Joyce, James: internationalism, 50, 160, 173; and language, 89; and politics, 165, 167; prose style, 87; *Finnegans Wake*, 13, 51, 66, 72, 162; *Ulysses*, 3, 11, 22, 28, 40–1, 66, 94, 120, 129, 158, 163

Jünger, Ernest, 166, 172

Kafka, Franz, 11; *The Castle*, 13

Kandinsky, Wassily, 104

Kant, Immanuel: *Critique of Judgement* (1790), 156–7;

184

INDEX

Critique of Pure Reason (1781), 107

Keats, John, 'To Autumn,' 106–7

Lacan, Jacques, 24

Larkin, Philip, 13

Lawrence, D.H.: alternative communities, 8; impersonality, 139, 141–2; internationalism, 46; reactionary politics, 167, 172; *The Rainbow*, 114; *Women in Love*, 41, 116, 163

Le Corbusier, 133

Leavis, F.R., 104

Lewis, Percy Wyndham, 11, 22, 160, 166

Lissitsky, El, 122

literacy and reading, growth of, 62–4

Lukács, Georg, 14; *The Meaning of Contemporary Realism*, 10

machine, and the avant-garde, 137–8

Malevich, Kazimir, 133

Mallarmé, Stéphane, 24, 94, 120, 165, 172

Mansfield, Katherine, 161–2

Marcuse, Herbert, 152

Marinetti, Filippo Tommaso, 131, 165

Márquez, Gabriel García, 7

Martyn, Edward, 53

Marx, Karl, 130–1; *Capital* (1867), 74–5

mass culture and literature, modernist dislike of, 63–4

Mayakovsky, Vladimir, 121, 122, 133, 134, 145, 147, 165

Merleau-Ponty, Maurice, 86

Meyerhold, Vsevolod, 121, 125, 138

Milton, John, 108

Moholy-Nagy, László, 123

Moore, George, 51, 53

Moore, Marianne, 18, 67, 99, 167

Moretti, Franco, 3

Morris, William, *News from Nowhere* (1890), 68

Moscow State Theatre, 121

Musil, Robert, *The Man Without Qualities* (1930–43), 91

Naipaul, V.S., 160

Neruda, Pablo, 104

newspapers, and the reading public, 62–4

Nietzsche, Friedrich, 9, 28, 72, 86, 168–9

O'Brien, Flann, 50

obscurity, 112–13

O'Casey, Seán, 165

Orwell, George, *Nineteen Eighty-Four* (1949), 95–6

Osborne, Peter, 39

phenomenology, 27, 120, 140

photography, and the avant-garde, 134–5

Pippin, Robert, 61

Piscator, Erwin, 123–4, 125, 132

Poggioli, Renato, *The Theory of the Avant-Garde*, 126

politics, and modernism, 165–72

Pope, Alexander, *The Dunciad*, 9

Popova, Lyubov, 133

popular press, expansion of, 62–4

post-colonialism, 44–6

185

INDEX

postmodernism, 2, 8, 11–12, 15, 25, 44

Pound, Ezra, 17, 20, 98, 99, 103, 166, 171; 'The Seafarer,' 13; *The Cantos*, 3, 72

propaganda, 156–7

Proust, Marcel: style and syntax, 93; *Remembrance of Things Past*, 27, 28, 87

Pushkin, Alexander, *Eugene Onegin*, 146

Rancière, Jacques, 94–5

realism, 10, 12–13

reception theory, 72

Red Review, The (play), 123

Reich, Wilhelm, 152

Richardson, Dorothy, 72, 92, 151; *Pilgrimage*, 26, 76, 86–7, 95, 120, 166

Rilke, Rainer Maria, 11, 128, 172

Rimbaud, Arthur, 14, 165

Robbe-Grillet, Alain, 97

Rodchenko, Aleksandr, 122, 134

Rushdie, Salman, 7, 161

Russian Formalists, 71, 101, 151

Russian Suprematists, 99, 122, 133

Russolo, Luigi, 98

Said, Edward, 164

Salford, agitprop theatre groups, 122

Sartre, Jean-Paul, 85–6; *What Is Literature?* (1948), 73

Schiller, Friedrich, *On the Aesthetic Education of Man* (1794), 157

Schmitt, Carl, 166

Schoenberg, Arnold, 6–7

Scholem, Gershom, 86

Scrutiny (journal), 104

Sebald, W.G., *Austerlitz* (2001), 81

Second World War, 5–6

Shakespeare, William, *Twelfth Night*, 89–90

Shklovsky, Viktor, 72, 102, 121

Shostakovich, Dmitri, 121

Simmel, Georg, 23, 59

Situationists, 15

socialist realism, 147

Soviet Union, and the avant-garde, 121–2, 125, 134–9, 143–7

Spengler, Oswald, *The Decline of the West*, 29

Stein, Gertrude: internationalism, 159; and language, 81, 99, 102; patronage, 68; reactionary politics, 167; *The Making of Americans* (1925), 74

Stepanova, Varvara, 133

Sterne, Laurence, *Tristram Shandy*, 15–16

Stevens, Wallace, 64, 85, 172

Stoker, Bram, 51

Stoppard, Tom, 161

stream of consciousness, 87

style and form, and 'high' art, 64–7

sublime, the, 95

Surrealists, 27, 71, 87, 99, 101, 119, 150–3

Swift, Jonathan, 53

Symbolism, 84–5, 100, 114

Synge, J.M., 42, 50, 51, 53, 54, 100

Tatlin, Vladimir, 122, 133, 135, 137

Taylorism, 137–8

Tennyson, Alfred, 109

INDEX

Thomas, Edward, 23
Trollope, Anthony, 161
Trotsky, Leon, 135, 153
Tzara, Tristan, 41

Valéry, Paul, 20, 76
Vertov, Dziga, 133

Weber, Max, 62
Weil, Simone, 141–2
Weill, Kurt, 123
West, Rebecca, 66
Wilde, Oscar, 47, 160, 165; 'The Critic as Artist' (1891), 115
Williams, Raymond, 8
Williams, William Carlos, 97, 103
Wittgenstein, Ludwig, 7
Wollen, Peter, 150
Woolf, Viriginia: and absences, 11; and British establishment, 46; and characteristics of modernism, 7; on Dorothy Richardson, 92; and the fluidity of the subject, 140; politics of, 167; style and syntax, 93–4; *A Room of One's Own* (1929), 165

Yeats, W.B.: archaisms, 42; and the elite, 158; and Irish modernism, 50–4; modernist characteristics, 8–9; as public poet, 9, 108–10; reactionary politics, 166, 172; and symbolism, 49, 83–5; and temporality, 28; and transcendence, 17; 'The Second Coming' (1919), 83

Žižek, Slavoj, 3
Zola, Émile, 66, 104